SECRET

FIRE

GW00480627

SECRET
FIRE

THE SPIRITUAL VISION
OF J. R. R. TOLKIEN

STRATFORD CALDECOTT

DARTON·LONGMAN+TODD

First published in 2003 by
Darton, Longman and Todd Ltd
1 Spencer Court
140–142 Wandsworth High Street
London SW18 4JJ

ISBN 0 232 52477 7

A catalogue record for this book is available from the British Library.

Designed by Sandie Boccacci
Phototypeset in 10.5/14pt Times New Roman
by Intype Libra Ltd
Printed and bound in Great Britain by
Page Bros, Norwich, Norfolk

CОПTEПTS

ACKNOWLEDGMENTS

Special thanks are due to my family, including my Elvish wife
Léonie and our daughters Teresa, Sophie and Rose-Marie. I am also
grateful to Carol and Phil Zaleski, Robert Murray SJ, Ben Kobus and
David Christopher Schindler for their helpful comments on parts of
the book. Fr Ian Boyd CSB has published several of my articles on
Tolkien in *The Chesterton Review* and has kindly given permission
to re-use some of that material here. One of those articles was first
given as a talk in Bath under the auspices of the Catholic Chaplain
to Higher Education, Fr William McLoughlin OSM, and subsequently
also appeared as 'The Heroism of Hobbits' in *Hidden Presence: The
Catholic Imagination of J. R. R. Tolkien* (Chesterton Press, 2003).
This and any other material based on articles that have appeared in
Epiphany, *Touchstone* magazine and the *Saint Austin Review* has
been thoroughly reworked for the present book. I am grateful to
HarperCollins Publishers Ltd for permission to quote copyright
passages from the works listed in the Bibliography and to the
Tolkien Estate for forcing me to keep these to a minimum. Finally, I
must thank Helen Porter and others at DLT for their care and
patience, and my editor, Brendan Walsh, for his encouragement as
the original deadline came and went.

iΠTRODUCTiOΠ

The Lord of the Rings (together with its prequel, *The Hobbit*) is said to have been the most widely-read book of the twentieth century after the Bible. An epic fantasy about the quest to destroy an evil Ring of Power, it appeals to people of all ages and beliefs, in a broad spectrum from Christian to neo-pagan. Its author, an Oxford don, was a devout Roman Catholic, but the majority of his readers are not aware of this. An understanding of J. R. R. Tolkien's personal beliefs and their influence on the story for which he is famous can only enhance our appreciation of this great work of art.

Ever since the Second World War, and certainly since the 1960s, the fashion among our intelligentsia has been to expose (or even exaggerate) the all-too-human side of the great and the famous: aristocrats, politicians, artists, explorers, scientists. However, the yearning for real heroism never dies. *The Lord of the Rings* is heroic saga on a grand scale, belonging to an ancient tradition of magical romances and legend. In his review C. S. Lewis paid it this tribute:

> The book is like lightning from a clear sky; as sharply different, as unpredictable in our age as *Songs of Innocence* were in theirs. To say that in it heroic romance, gorgeous, eloquent, and unashamed, has suddenly returned at a period almost pathological in its anti-romanticism, is inadequate . . . It marks not a return but an advance or revolution: the conquest of new territory. Nothing quite like it was ever done before.[1]

The Lord of the Rings was an advance because it was not merely heroic, nor merely romantic. Though permeated with a kind of

[1]

nostalgia, it was a thoroughly modern work. Tom Shippey compares it to the work of William Golding, George Orwell and T. H. White, all of whom wrote fantasy as a way of struggling with evils that had been exposed by the great twentieth-century wars. Their writing was 'modern' because it was deeply marked by this experience. Millions of human beings died on the fields of France, in Russia, in the death camps of Germany, in the fire-bombing of Dresden, in the nuclear conflagration of Hiroshima and Nagasaki. By the time of Tolkien's death in 1973, a moral miasma had settled over the spirits of the English, as the disillusionment and the compromises of the century began to take their toll.

What the book celebrates – and mourns – is a world and a tradition that appears to be passing away in a great war, or series of wars. These wars are fought in a good cause, against an enemy that cannot be allowed to win. Yet the real danger is not that the free world might be defeated; it is that we might be corrupted, brutalised and degraded by the conflict itself, and in particular by the means employed to secure victory. Tolkien always denied that Mordor was intended as a representation of Nazi Germany, or Soviet Russia, but was quite aware of its 'applicability' to the death camps and the gulags, to Fascism and Communism – as well as to other, more subtle or fragmentary manifestations of the same spirit.

Of course, the point is partly that the allies against Sauron resisted the temptation to use the Ring against its maker, and as a result the War of the Ring could be the prelude to a new Golden Age in Middle-earth, a civilisation of love, justice and peace. And yet even in the War of the Ring (as the opening of the film version reminds us), much that was beautiful departed and is now forgotten. Our mistake in the great wars of our own time has been to accept the false idea that the end justifies the means, and that 'if a thing can be done, it must be done'(*Letters* 186[2]). For, as Tolkien wrote to his son in 1944, the Allies were attempting to defeat Sauron by using the Ring. The penalty would be to breed new Saurons, and to turn Men and Elves into Orcs – 'Not that in real life things are as clear cut as in a story, and we started with a great many Orcs on our side'(L 66).

M O П S T E R S A П D C R İ T İ C S

Tolkien's importance as a post-war writer who used fantasy to explore profound moral and spiritual themes was not recognised when *The Lord of the Rings* was first published in the 1950s. Back in 1936, the subtitle of Tolkien's academic paper on *Beowulf*, 'The Monsters and the Critics', had half jokingly implied that the literary critics of the Old English poem which Tolkien loved were adversaries of the hero, perhaps even akin to monsters themselves. And so, when *The Lord of the Rings* did appear in print, Tolkien knew pretty much what to expect. In fact, it was derided by a number of critics on both sides of the Atlantic, Edmund Wilson famously describing it as 'juvenile trash'.

The reason often given for despising the novel was that 'good' and 'bad' were so clearly delineated that the plot was simplistic and childish. But, as we have just seen, Tolkien was well aware of the complexity and muddle of real life – and yet held his writing to be 'realistic', indeed truer to the inner life than most of the supposedly 'grown up' novels the critics had in mind (see L 71).

Tolkien drew upon a much older tradition of storytelling than the modern novel, with its typically materialistic assumptions. He was retrieving the art of mythological or *mythopoeic* thinking, which is as old as mankind itself, and deeply entwined with our religious sense. The book appeals to universal constants in human nature, constants that are reflected in traditional mythology and folklore the world over. Mythological thinking does not provide an 'escape' from reality so much as an 'intensification' of it, as another fantasy writer (Alan Garner) once rightly said. It is this that in part explains the novel's wide appeal – and also the contempt it aroused among those whose world-view and mindset are closed in advance against all such uses of the imagination.

The Lord of the Rings may be read, therefore, as an exciting story that spectacularly revives an almost-extinct literary genre. But it can also be enjoyed in other ways: as an extended meditation on what it means to be English, or as an imaginative response to the experience of modern warfare, or as a moving evocation of the intimate relationship between love and heroism. As we shall see, it can be read, too, as an exploration of the roots of human language and consciousness. Most strangely of all, perhaps, it can be viewed as a deliberate experiment in a kind of *time travel* using dreams and 'linguistic ghosts' to overcome the limitations of individual memory and experience.

When the first volume of *The Lord of the Rings* was published Tolkien wrote in trepidation that 'I have exposed my heart to be shot at'. The themes of his writing are the keys to Tolkien's own deepest concerns, including death and immortality, nostalgia for paradise, creation and creativity, the reality of virtue and sin, the right stewardship of nature, and the moral dangers posed by the possession of technological power. By wrestling with these concerns he created a body of work that is imbued with a profound wisdom – a wisdom that our civilisation desperately needs – drawn very largely from the Catholic faith in which he was raised. Of course, he was not writing dogmatic theology, even in the letters and commentaries where he came closest to explaining what he was about. But because he *believed* in the truth of certain dogmas, these acted for him like torches or crystalline lamps that transmit light into dark places. It was with the light they transmitted and what it might reveal that he was concerned in his own work, not directly with the fashioning of the lamps themselves: he was humble enough to leave that to the professionals. His spirituality is that unpretentious 'spirituality of the everyday' that we find in many of the most popular Catholic authors, such as Jean-Pierre de Caussade or Thérèse of Lisieux. The hobbits exemplify this humility and everyday-ness which is at the heart of his writing.

Thus, while the reader is never assumed to be a Christian believer, the cosmological setting of Tolkien's imagined world, along with the creatures and events with which he filled it and the moral laws governing this imagined cosmos, were all intended to be compatible with his beliefs about reality, and in fact provide 'pointers' to a Christian world-view. Love, courage, justice, mercy, kindness, integrity and the other virtues are incarnated in the story through characters such as Aragorn and Frodo. It is a testimony to the power and realism of the Christian tradition that exposure to these patterns of the moral life can have a purifying effect on the receptive reader, yet without making us feel confined or oppressed within an ideological system. Many return to *The Lord of the Rings* again and again for refreshment of soul – perhaps even for the kind of healing that the author must have experienced in the writing of it.

My exploration of Tolkien's vision will draw upon the stories themselves, along with the 'History of Middle-Earth' edited from Tolkien's papers by his son Christopher, but also upon the published *Letters*, Tolkien's own essays, short stories and poems, and some of the best critical and biographical works that have appeared in the last few years. The title hardly needs explaining to anyone who has read *The Lord of the Rings*, or seen the Peter Jackson movie. Gandalf the wizard names himself a 'servant of the Secret Fire' during his confrontation with the Balrog in Moria, and he is in fact later revealed as the bearer of the elvish Ring of Fire, Narya the Great. But the fire he serves is not simply that of the ring he bears. Fire is a much bigger and more complex theme in the stories than that. Indeed, the secret fire is at the heart not just of *The Lord of the Rings*, but of the wider tapestry of stories sometimes known as 'the *legendarium*' or 'the Silmarillion' (I will use the latter in italics only when I am referring to the published book of that title). Let us now go in search of Tolkien's secret fire, which the Enemy also sought but failed to find, 'for it is with Ilúvatar'.

I

THE TREE OF TALES

Tolkien was an explorer. The stories in which he invested so much time and energy are notes of his expeditions in search of an older or 'inner' world. Over the years he added revision after revision, layer by layer, working late into the night, filling in a vast historical canvas, weaving theme upon theme, until the whole collection resembled a great 'tree of tales', like the gnarled oaks he loved.

Now that we have access to the vast corpus of unfinished and reworked stories and background material, thanks to his son Christopher's labours on the twelve-volume 'History of Middle-Earth', we can see how much time and energy went into this writing. If his contemporaries and peers had known the full scale of his enterprise, they would have been shocked. What drove Tolkien so late into the night was not merely the obsession to tell a story, but the belief that 'legends and myths are largely made of "truth", and indeed present aspects of it that can only be perceived in this mode' (L 131). He knew he was writing fiction, but at the same time he felt that he was *telling the truth* about the world as it revealed itself to him. And this truth he discovered as he wrote, through the very process of writing. He claimed always to have had the sense that he was recording what was already 'there', rather than inventing stuff out of his own head (L 131); a feeling that lay behind the fictional device of the 'Red Book of Westmarch' on which *The Lord of the Rings* itself pretended to be based. In a letter to Christopher he admitted that the story seemed almost to write itself, and sometimes took a direction very different from the preliminary sketch, as if the truth was trying to emerge through him (L 91). In some sense, then, he did actually believe what he was writing. ('There are secondary planes or degrees,' he writes in the 'Notion Club Papers'.)

His stories were set not in a distant galaxy or another world, but in this world a long time ago. In a draft letter to an admirer dated 1971 (L 328), Tolkien described writing with great care for detail, so as to produce a 'picture' that would appear to be set against a limitless background, with infinite extensions through both time and space. Each particular element of the story had to appear to belong to a much larger and more ancient body of literature, in order to evoke the symbolic resonances without which it would fail to cast its spell. There had to be a sense of great vistas around and behind each story, as there is in the legends of a people like the Norsemen or the Celts, each of which comes down to us out of its own tremendous 'mythic space'.

But what follows in the same letter is especially interesting. It seems to suggest that, while he could analyse to some extent what he was doing and why, and how he achieved the literary effects he did, he was at the same time extremely puzzled by what had been given to him – that he felt a mystery at work. He goes on:

> Looking back on the wholly unexpected things that have followed its publication . . . I feel as if an ever darkening sky over our present world had been suddenly pierced, the clouds rolled back, and an almost forgotten sunlight had poured down again. As if indeed the horns of Hope had been heard again, as Pippin heard them suddenly at the absolute *nadir* of the fortunes of the West. But *How?* and *Why?* (L 328)

This sense of mystery is deepened by an encounter in real life with a figure he identifies as Gandalf, in the person of a man who visited him to discuss certain old pictures that seemed almost designed to illustrate *The Lord of the Rings*, but which Tolkien had never before seen. The man remarks after a silence: 'Of course you don't suppose, do you, that you wrote all that book yourself?' Tolkien goes on:

> Pure Gandalf! I was too well acquainted with G. to expose myself rashly, or to ask what he meant. I think I said: 'No, I don't suppose so any longer.' I have never since been able to suppose so. An alarming conclusion for an old philologist to draw concerning his private amusement. But not one that should puff any one up who considers the imperfections of 'chosen instruments', and indeed what sometimes seems their lamentable unfitness for the purpose.

A 'chosen instrument'? I don't want to make too much of this, but the letter is revealing. Tolkien seems to have felt that it had been given to him to sound the horn of hope in a darkling world, and those many thousands of readers who return again and again to the book and film for refreshment of soul might well agree with him. This is a story that tells us things we need to know. It cannot be taken in all at once. It is one of those that we have to *grow into*; stories that deal with the way the world is made, and the way the self is made. These stories are like dreams, but dreams that can be shared by an entire culture; wholesome dreams that restore a balance to the psyche by turning our energies and our thoughts towards truth; dreams that resemble an oasis in the desert. Reading them can be a meditation. Why is that? This is the question I want to answer.

THE HALL OF FİRE

J. R. R. Tolkien was born in Bloemfontein, South Africa, in 1892 and lived there until the age of three. Then for reasons of health his mother Mabel brought him and his brother back to England, settling in a beautiful corner of rural Warwickshire. His father, Arthur Tolkien, was supposed to join them later, but died before the family were reunited.

When Mabel became a Roman Catholic in 1900 she was cut off

by her mixed Anglican, Baptist and Unitarian family and reduced to poverty. She was forced to move from the countryside into the town, and there she was taken under the wing of Father Francis Morgan CO, a priest of the Oratory of St Philip Neri in Birmingham (a religious community whose English branch had been founded by John Henry Newman fifty years earlier). It was Fr Morgan who helped to look after the family and provided spiritual guidance.

Tolkien was only twelve when his mother died of diabetes, worn out (he later wrote) by the poverty that was a direct result of her conversion to Catholicism, and Fr Morgan became the boy's guardian. Thus it was that he grew to manhood under the protection and guidance of an exemplary Catholic priest. All his life he tried to attend Mass daily, finding in it a constant source of strength and grace.

Thereafter the story of his life might be presented under three main headings. The first of these would be *Romance*. He falls in love at the age of sixteen with the nineteen-year-old Edith Bratt, but is not allowed by his priest-guardian to propose to her until he comes of age five years later. Edith having by then consented to be received into the Catholic Church, they are married in Warwick just before Tolkien sets off with the Lancashire Fusiliers to fight the Germans in the First World War. Only when he returns are they able to live happily as man and wife. The image he has of her is always that of a young beauty dancing among the hemlocks in a forest glade near Roos in Yorkshire, close to the military camp where Tolkien was stationed in 1917: it is one of the seeds of his writing, for it becomes the encounter between his hero Beren and the Elven princess Lúthien – echoed also in the story of Aragorn and Arwen which, though it is mainly found in the Appendices of *The Lord of the Rings*, Tolkien regarded as a vital element of the story.

Heading number two: *War*. The earliest beginnings of the written mythology date from 1914, the year Britain entered the First World War, although Tolkien was allowed to finish his studies at Oxford in 1915 before military training. He survives the war through the 'luck' of being sent back from the Somme with trench fever. As he recovers, he writes the first sustained fragment of the Silmarillion, 'The Fall of Gondolin'. Most of his male friends are killed within a few years, and he is awed by the heroism of the ordinary English soldier. That heroism will find its way into *The Lord of the Rings*, into the hobbits, and the figure of Sam Gamgee in particular. Published in 1954–55, the whole novel is a tribute to the spirit of ordinary, decent men who died for their country in the Great War, and it was largely composed during the Second World War, in the face of the later, almost demonic evil unleashed on the world by Adolf Hitler.

The third heading is *Oxford*, where Tolkien becomes Professor of Anglo-Saxon in 1925, and forms the Kolbitár (Coalbiter) reading group devoted to the Icelandic sagas, which later merges with – or takes over – the Inklings in the 1930s. The influence of this real-life fellowship on his writing cannot be overestimated: without it he would have lacked the encouragement or confidence to continue. The friendship of C. S. Lewis in particular, whom he helped to convert to Christianity, played a crucial role, as did that of George Sayer, who at one point revived his determination to find a publisher.

Much has been written on the Inklings over the years as the fame of Lewis and Tolkien spread around the world, not least an important study by Humphrey Carpenter, Tolkien's biographer. I will not try to summarise it all here: as with the details of Tolkien's life, the facts are easily available. Tolkien influenced Lewis's conversion to Christianity, though the latter perhaps never overcame his remaining Ulster prejudices sufficiently to become a Catholic. The other members of the group were an even more varied bunch, ranging from Charles Williams the High-Church Anglican with his mystical and somewhat unorthodox ideas about love and magic, to Owen Barfield the Anthroposophist with an interest in language and the evolution of consciousness. Anyone who has lived in Oxford, and attended the pubs where the group often met, will be able to picture the scene – pints of bitter wreathed in smoke, loud conversation (especially from Lewis), ancient languages, fragments of story and new poems intoned, frequent interruptions, critical comment and laughter.

I sometimes think of the Inklings when I read the description of Elrond's 'Hall of Fire' in Rivendell, for it is there that they would have been most at home. The hall was a constant element in Tolkien's writing, its first appearance being the Room of the Log Fire in a story he wrote back in 1916–17 called 'The Cottage of Lost Play', where 'old tales, old songs, and elfin music are treasured and rehearsed'.

It is easy to idealise the Inklings, but the reality was often humdrum enough, with its fair share of frustration and human weakness. Members came and went, and in the end even Tolkien and Lewis fell out somewhat, partly over Lewis's marriage to a divorcee, to which Tolkien, as a devout Catholic, took exception. Perhaps, as some allege, there may have been some jealousy on Tolkien's part of Lewis's apparently easy success with the Narnia stories, which he thought overly clumsy and allegorical (L 265), and of Lewis's friendship with Charles Williams (this by his own admission in L 252, 257, 259).

Nevertheless, the friendships among 'the brotherhood' were real and deep, and many moments of intense communion more than made up for the occasional tensions. Lewis never ceased to praise Tolkien's work, even during the period of estrangement, and for his part Tolkien was deeply shaken by Lewis's death in 1963, writing: 'this feels like an axe-blow near the roots. Very sad that we should have been so separated in the last years; but our time of close communion endured in memory for both of us' (L 251). For many years, Lewis had been Tolkien's only audience for what might have remained, but for this, a private hobby (L 276).

But although *The Lord of the Rings* may have depended on the encouragement of Lewis (combined with the success of Tolkien's children's story *The Hobbit*) to get it going, the secret life that was to feed into it was well underway before the Inklings ever started to read to each other in the Bird and Baby, and long before Tolkien wrote the famous academic essays which summed up his thoughts on literature, 'Beowulf: The Monsters and the Critics' (1936) and 'On

Fairy-Stories' (1939). It was underway even before the war that marked him permanently with the experience of great evil and suffering. The seeds of that secret life lie back in his childhood, and especially in the happy days he spent playing with his brother Hilary in the countryside around Sarehole (the inspiration for Hobbiton), and in the intimations of 'beauty and majesty' he received in the Catholic Mass.

GOING 'INSIDE LANGUAGE'

From his earliest introduction to Church Latin by his mother he loved languages, and quickly began to make up some of his own. Through the study of languages, a whole range of other influences began to reach him. Eventually Tolkien was to master many European tongues, both ancient and modern, but he always retained a particular affection for Latin, Gothic, Welsh and Finnish. He loved poetry more than prose, probably because it expressed the rhythms and character of each language in purest form. The 'Sister Songs' of the mystical Victorian Catholic poet Francis Thompson may have helped kindle his love of elves, but in 1912 he began to study Finnish, and here he tells us he found the seeds of Quenya, the High-Elvish of his own invention. He once wrote to W. H. Auden of the pleasure he experienced reading a Finnish Grammar in Exeter College library, when he was supposed to be revising for an exam: 'It was like discovering a complete wine-cellar filled with bottles of an amazing wine of a kind and flavour never tasted before' (L163).

It was the mystique of Northern Europe (which he sometimes called 'Northernness') that particularly appealed to him, a spirit that he felt in the Norse or Icelandic sagas, for example the 'Prophecy of the Seeress' in the Elder Edda concerning the beginning and end of the world. He believed that the mythology of his own land in particular had been lost or destroyed (or overlayed by Celtic and French influences). It needed to be recovered in something of the way Nikolaj Grundtvig had compiled Danish and Norwegian legends in the nineteenth century, or Snorri Sturluson the Icelandic *Prose Edda* in the thirteenth. Both men had been Christians trying to preserve what they saw as enriching or beautiful in pagan material.

Just as influential, and very much an inspiration to Tolkien, was Elias Lönnrot, a Lutheran Christian who reconstituted Finnish folklore from surviving oral and runic traditions during the nineteenth century. It is generally agreed that Lönnrot's *Kalevala* played a crucial role in the development of Finnish national identity, consolidated when Finland achieved independence at the end of 1917. Rudolf Steiner, the founder of the Anthroposophical Society and later to be a major influence on Owen Barfield, lectured on the *Kalevala* in Helsinki in 1912, believing it to be one of Europe's great sacred texts, the vehicle of a secret wisdom. For Tolkien it represented the possibility of a 'good paganism' compatible with Christianity. Probably in the same year that Steiner was lecturing, Tolkien began to work on the *Kalevala*, and to adapt some of its themes and characters into stories of his own (the tragic hero Kullervo, mingled with Sigurd and Oedipus from other sources, became Túrin in *Unfinished Tales*).

Then there was Anglo-Saxon. This was the language that had come to maturity in eighth-century Northumbria, at the confluence of two movements of Christian missionaries, from north and south: the Celtic monks from Ireland and Iona to Lindisfarne, and the Benedictines from Canterbury to York, Wearmouth and Jarrow. For two golden centuries, before the devastation wrought by the Vikings, a Christian civilisation blossomed in the north of England which proved capable of assimilating the best traditions of paganism and raising them to a new cultural level. The monasteries were islands or oases of culture, producing great works of art like the Lindisfarne Gospels, with their earthy humour and sinuous, interlaced decoration. The English language of that time achieved a maturity that is exemplified by great works such as the *Dream of the Rood* and, of course, *Beowulf*, which Tolkien translated and on which he wrote his most influential scholarly essay. At least one commentator (Bradley

J. Birzer) has likened these monasteries, with their great libraries and lore-masters, such as the Venerable Bede and Alcuin, who became the 'schoolmaster of Europe' under Charlemagne, to Rivendell and Lothlórien, and Gandalf to the Anglo-Saxon missionary St Boniface, defending civilisation from the barbarians of the East.

By 1914 Tolkien had encountered a poem of this period by Cynewulf called *Crist* ('Christ'). Two lines of the poem struck him in a way he never forgot:

> *Éalá Éarendel engla beorhtast*
> *ofer middangeard monnum sended!*
> Hail Earendel, brightest of angels,
> above the middle-earth sent unto men!

Tolkien describes the first impact of the poem upon him in the voice of the character Lowdham in his 'Notion Club Papers' (about which more in a moment):

> 'When I came across that citation in the dictionary I felt a curious thrill, as if something had stirred in me, half wakened from sleep. There was something very remote and strange and beautiful behind those words, if I could grasp it, far beyond ancient English . . . I don' t think it is any irreverence to say that it may derive its curiously moving quality from some older world.'

Tolkien, like Lowdham in the story, went in search of that older world. He believed certain vivid dreams could grant access to it. (He often mentions a recurrent 'Atlantis dream' of a great wave drowning a green landscape, which he remembers from his earliest years in South Africa, and which his son also later experienced.) The other way back to the past was through language itself, and 'linguistic ghosts' that are traces and vestiges of the ancient world in modern speech or names. At the end of his life, the obituary composed for *The Times* some years earlier by C. S. Lewis described Tolkien as having travelled in some sense 'inside language'. It is a powerful phrase, and a true one. Verlyn Flieger records the question put to Tolkien once by a fellow philologist: 'You broke the veil, didn't you, and passed through?' He 'readily admitted' having done so. For him language itself had an interior: by penetrating within it, he found himself entering the same imaginal world to which his special dreams were pointing. In fact, the 'older world' is a world both ancient and interior, which is precisely what we mean by *mythic.*

By the end of the long vacation of 1914, Tolkien was staying at Phoenix Farm in Nottinghamshire. There he wrote a poem, the first fruit of his meditations on the mysterious verse from Cynewulf. It was called 'The Voyage of Earendel the Evening Star', and it was the beginning of all that is most original in Tolkien's mythology. You will find the most developed form of it at the heart of *The Fellowship of the Ring*: it is the song composed by Bilbo (with a little help from Aragorn) that Frodo hears, half in a dream, in the Hall of Fire in Elrond's house, and it begins as follows:

> Eärendil was a mariner
> that tarried in Arvernien;
> he built a boat of timber felled
> in Nimbrethil to journey in;
> her sails he wove of silver fair,
> of silver were her lanterns made,
> her prow was fashioned like a swan,
> and light upon her banners laid . . .

It goes on to describe how the Mariner (father of Elrond Half-Elven and distant ancestor of Aragorn) achieves his mission in the Undying Lands, and being forbidden to set foot again in Middle-earth is sent by the Immortals to journey for ever in a silver, winged ship across the shoreless skies, shining now and for ever as the brightest star above Middle-earth, the 'star' we know as Venus, herald of the dawn and the evening. The earliest version of the poem may be found in *The Book of Lost Tales* (Part II), together with an account of its evolution. It began as follows:

Éarendel arose where the shadow flows
at Ocean's silent brim;
through mouth of night as a ray of light
where the shores are sheer and dim
he launched his bark like a silver spark
from the last and lonely sand;
then on sunlit breath of day's fiery death
he sailed from Westerland . . .

If this is close to the heart of Tolkien's poetic vision of the cosmos, it also illustrates the importance of language, of the sound of words, of poetry, for the inner journey that he was engaged in. The 'curious thrill' he speaks of is not evoked purely by the sound of the individual words used by Cynewulf, but by their setting in a poetic context, which gives them their musical quality and ability to touch the heart. The phrase in question may be from an explicitly Christian poem, but Tolkien does not immediately jump to an explicitly Christian interpretation (L 297). Nor is he satisfied by the easily available (to him) Germanic and Old Norse references to a star or messenger of this name. These only intrigued him further.

What interests him is primarily the ancient world, the mythic history, evoked by the phrase. He sees this phrase employed by the poet as imbued with a kind of race memory that he wants to spend much of his life recovering, or helping to regenerate. From this fragment, removed from its context in the poem as a whole, and combined with other clues and evidence, he senses the possibility of rebuilding the long-lost mythology of pre-Norman England (L 131 and 180).

Language remained the key to this reconstruction, and a glance at the theories of fellow-Inkling Owen Barfield can help us understand how. For Barfield, the development of consciousness, mythology and language go hand in hand. He believed that human language and

[17]

consciousness have evolved together from a state of 'original participation', in which subject and object, word and thing, were virtually
identified, to a state of alienation in which they are separated to such
a degree that the sense of connectedness – with nature and with each
other – has been lost. The earlier form of consciousness expressed
itself primarily in myth, in poetry and metaphor. Ancient language
used images of things to express its meaning. Later, with the development of abstract thought, metaphor falls into the background, and
for a scientific consciousness detachment and measurement become
all-important. This is a necessary stage in the emergence of a new
kind of participation, a conscious communion with all things her-
alded in human evolution (or so Barfield thought, following Steiner)
by the appearance of Christ.

The opposite of abstract thought, Barfield tells us, is symbolic
thought or imagination. Following Coleridge, he divides *phantasie*
into two, on the one hand 'fancy' or the mere image-making capacity,
and on the other 'imagination', which is a creative and perceptive
power. (Tolkien prefers to call the higher faculty 'Fantasy', so his
terminology is reversed but the basic idea is the same.)

Myth-making or *mythopoeia*, for all the Inklings, is an act of the
creative imagination. It is closely related to the poetic roots of language itself. Naming is not merely the attachment of arbitrary labels
to things, but involves us in the imaginative/intellectual grasping of
what they are. To give a name to something is to therefore pick it out
from its context, to identify it as a thing-in-itself, and to perceive at
least something of its character and purpose in relation to ourselves.
Poetry takes this to another level. It discovers the things revealed in
experience to be analogies, similes, metaphors, symbols, each in
some sense pregnant with inexhaustible meaning. We 'know' things
more completely by finding the connection between one thing and
another, and between myself and all those things, in a way that illu-
minates both.

The study of etymology, of the origins and evolution of word-
forms, could therefore be a journey back in time and consciousness,

for the words themselves – and especially the concrete metaphors they were originally based upon – bear traces of original participation. Readers of *The Lord of the Rings* will recall the words of Treebeard to Merry and Pippin: 'Real names tell you the story of the things they belong to in my language.'

THE ΠOTiOΠ CLUB

Some of Tolkien's unfinished stories give us further insights into his attempts to explore the past through language. The 'Notion Club Papers' are an example, and are especially worth reading because the Notion Club was closely modelled on his experience of the Inklings (though he warns us against identifying them too closely, calling it a 'cracked mirror'). The second part of the Papers were once labelled 'Beyond Lewis, or, Out of the Talkative Planet', and aspects of Tolkien's own self-portrait are evident in the character of Michael George Ramer, the Professor of Finno-Ugric Philology who is 'better known as a writer of romances'.

The Papers or 'minutes' of the Club were supposed to have been discovered around 2012 and to date from the 1980s. They begin with a discussion of science fiction (including the stories of H. G. Wells, C. S. Lewis and Olaf Stapleton), and then Ramer leads the Club – and especially Lowdham – into what proves to be a dangerous experiment. Believing that in certain 'serious dreams, or visions' we have access to memories and experiences not our own, he claims to have trained himself to 'travel' out of his body in this manner. Some of the glimpses he reports are thinly-disguised experiences of Tolkien himself, such as the green wave, the tall tower by the sea, and tall, slender trees crowned with blue and gold standing on a green mound (Lothlórien?). Beyond these dreams lay something even more mystical:

> But out of some place beyond the region of dreams, now and again there comes a blessedness, and it soaks through all the

[19]

levels, and illumines all the scenes through which the mind passes out back into waking, and so it flows out into this life. There it lasts long, but not forever in this world, and memory cannot reach its source. Often we ascribe it to the pictures seen on the margin radiant in its light, as we pass by and out. But a mountain far in the North caught in a slow sunset is not the Sun.

Ramer's journeys take him to alien worlds, far beyond Earth (the Talkative Planet) and the rest of our solar system, which he experiences as barren of life. Eshúrizel, home of the En-keladim: an inorganic world full of music, resembling a 'garden, a paradise of water, metal, stone, like the interwoven variations of vast natural orders of flowers'. Minal-Zidar the golden: 'absolutely silent and quiescent, a whole small world of one single perfect form, complete, imperishable in Time, finished, at peace, a jewel, a visible word, a realization in material form of contemplation and adoration'.

The members of the Club are particularly intrigued by the *names* Ramer comes up with, which he claims belong to his 'native language'. By this Ramer means what he calls 'Old Human, or Primitive Adamic'; that is, the first language of men.

> 'In language-invention, though you may seem to build only out of material taken from other acquired tongues, it is those elements most near to your native style that you select. In such rare dreams as I was thinking about, far away by oneself in voiceless countries, then your own native language bubbles up, and makes new names for strange new things.'

The Elvish En-keladim show Ramer the history of Atlantis in the 'Drama of the Silver Tree'.

> '[They are] sitting round in a circle and singing in that strange, long, long, but never-wearying, uncloying music, endlessly unfolding out of itself, while the song takes visible life among them. The Green Sea flowers in foam, and the Isle

rises and opens like a rose in the midst of it. There the Tree
opens the starred turf like a silver spear, and grows, and there
is a New Light; and the leaves unfold and there is Full Light;
and the leaves fall and there is a Rain of Light. Then the Door
opens – but no! I have no words for that Fear.'

The Club discusses the relationship of myth to history. Jeremy
suggests that ancient legends about 'the origins of kings, laws, and
the fundamental crafts' are not wholly inventions, or at least not
mere 'fiction': they have more *roots*. 'Roots in what?' asks Frankley.

'In Being, I think I should say,' Jeremy answered; 'and in
human Being; and coming down the scale, in the springs of
History and in the designs of Geography – I mean, well, in
the pattern of our world as it uniquely is, and of the events in
it as seen from a distance. A sort of parallel to the fact that
from far away the Earth would be seen as a revolving sunlit
globe; and that is a remote truth of enormous effect on us and
all we do, though not immediately discernible on earth,
where practical men are quite right in regarding the surface as
flat and immovable for practical purposes.'

Notice how Tolkien turns the tables on the 'practical men' – in this
case academic historians. Their scientific mentality is being compared here with flat-earthism. He goes on to refine his theory:

'Of course, the pictures presented by the legends may be
partly symbolical, they may be arranged in designs that com-
press, expand, foreshorten, combine, and are not at all realistic or photographic; yet they may tell you something true
about the Past.

'And mind you, there are also real details, what are called
facts, accidents of land-shape and sea-shape, of individual
men and their actions, that are caught up: the grains on which
the stories crystallize like snowflakes. There was a man
called Arthur at the centre of the cycle.'

Frankley objects that the Arthurian romances are not 'real in the same way as true past events are real'. Jeremy replies: 'I didn't say *in the same way* . . . There are secondary planes or degrees.'

In the Platonic-Romantic tradition of European literature there are many levels of reality. A 'Great Chain of Being' stretches from the pure spirits and empyrean spheres of imperishable crystal down to the changeable realms below the moon. Tolkien is exploring the possible application of this medieval cosmology to time, in a way that would reconcile the truths of science with the truths he has discerned in mythology. In effect, he was doing nothing less than developing a theory of myth that would account for his own ongoing, lifelong project, the Silmarillion.

In the story, the Club dwells on the experience of Númenor/ Atlantis. Lowdham is not a 'seer' like Ramer, but from the age of ten has experienced linguistic ghosts that connect him back to the events that Ramer has glimpsed. His real name turns out to be Ælfwine ('Elf-friend'), and his father Edwin an explorer who disappeared into the western ocean in a ship called *The Éarendel*. The fact that the final link back to Númenor/Atlantis is provided by a line of fathers and sons is highly significant, for the pattern recurs throughout the Silmarillion. The names Ælfwine, Errol, Eriol, Alboin, Alwin, Edwin and Elendil all mean 'Elf-friend'. Descendants of the first Elendil have the 'sea-longing', the haunting desire to travel back to the West.

Together the members of the Club discover that in its last days Númenor – Westernesse or 'the Land of Gift' – was corrupted by an evil force called *Zigūr* (Sauron in *The Lord of the Rings*). Attempting to wrest the secret of immortality from the gods by force, the evil Númenoreans provoke their own destruction. This is when the Papers, too, take a dramatic turn, as the mythic reality the Club is exploring starts to influence the world around them. Their recollection of the downfall of Númenor overshadowed by the eagles of the true Lords of the West causes a great storm to originate in the Atlantic Ocean, a storm which 'slew more men, felled more trees, and cast down more towers, bridges and other works of Man than a hundred years of wild weather.' Rather spookily, since he was writing in 1945, Tolkien places this fictional storm in the year 1987, which was in fact the year of a great storm that many in England and France still remember.

The story is not yet over – Tolkien goes on to connect it with the legends of St Brendan's Voyage and a journey by Lowdham to Ireland in pursuit of his father – but it was never completed. Interrupted by the need to get the final volume of *The Lord of the Rings* ready for publication, Tolkien never returned to the manuscript, or to the continued development of the Avallonian and Adunaic languages discovered by Lowdham.

We may regret that Tolkien never finished the story, but the Papers had become too chaotic, and in any case they seemed to have fulfilled their purpose, by clarifying in his mind the events surrounding the end of Númenor. The energies he would have used in making a publishable story out of the Papers were poured first into the Appendices of *The Lord of the Rings*, and then back into the wider waters of the Silmarillion.

It took all the dedication and scholarship of his son Christopher to bring this work into sufficient order to be publishable as *The Silmarillion*, four years after the author's death. But ironically one of the important elements that was lost in the transition was the explicit acknowledgment of the link between father and son in the discovery of the past. The only trace of Ælfwine that remains is Elendil, who now provides a suitably distinguished lineage for Aragorn. Yet Tolkien's filial piety was intense. He once wrote: 'The link between father and son is not only of the perishable flesh: it must have something of *aeternitas* about it' (L 45). His own father, Arthur, was taken from him by death when he was only four years old, soon after he and his mother had crossed the Atlantic Ocean separating England from South Africa. It is not hard to connect Tolkien's longing for the father in the far-away country he could barely remember with the sea-longing expressed in his stories, and to link this with the desire for an ancient world that has been taken away in a time before memory.

This is not an attempt to 'explain' the stories, although it may help to account for some of their poignancy. Nevertheless, it gives another level of meaning to a sentence I have quoted in passing: 'There was a man called Arthur at the centre of the cycle.' Tolkien's relationship to his own father became for him a mystical link to the past, to his own past and the past of the race, to the collective unconscious, the roots of the tree of tales. This link between generations, through which life and hope is transmitted from father to son, is also the way back through memory and language from the present world to a world that can be accurately described only in myth.

TREE AND LEAF

In the introductory note he wrote for the 1964 edition of *Tree and Leaf* (comprising the famous essay 'On Fairy-Stories' and the short story 'Leaf by Niggle'), Tolkien mentioned a 'great-limbed poplar tree' that had served as his inspiration for his short story.

> It was suddenly lopped and mutilated by its owner, I do not know why. It is cut down now, a less barbarous punishment for any crimes it may have been accused of, such as being large and alive. I do not think it had any friends, or any mourners, except myself and a pair of owls.

This was something more than sentimentality. It was not that he was literally reading human feelings or consciousness into the tree (or the owls!), but that tree was *present* and *alive* to him in a way it is not to most other people. Tolkien saw natural things freighted with the depth of meaning that all things possess, being rooted in the mind of God. God does not create things simply to fill up space. He creates for a reason, and the ultimate reason for his creation is love. Each thing, and especially each living thing, is a word, a symbol, a revelation. Each is a note, or a theme, in some great music. At any rate, it is more than itself: that is, more than the thing most people see when they look at it.

The symbolic properties of the tree have been obvious to many people and cultures. Jewish and Christian Scriptures place a tree or trees at the centre of Paradise. The Norse legends that Tolkien loved speak of the World Tree *Yggdrasil* whose trunk runs through the heart of Middle-earth. Yggdrasil is great Ash, whose branches support the Nine Worlds and reach to the heavens above Asgard. Its roots reach down to Hel, at its foot is a fountain of wisdom, and upon it the father-god Odin (Woden) hung wounded for nine days and nights before achieving a knowledge of the Mysteries and his own resurrection. 'Middle-earth' (Midgard) gets its name, obviously, from its position between heaven and hell.

The tree of tales, similarly, links all the worlds, and is the source of wisdom for those who hang upon it. The way a tree grows – slowly, incrementally, organically – is the way myths and legends grow, the way a tradition grows. It is the way Tolkien's *legendarium* grew. There may be sudden spurts of growth in good weather, boughs may be lopped off or felled by a storm, there may be seasons when the tree wears green, or bursts forth in flower or fruit, but at all times there is a sap and a spirit that runs through it and makes it a living thing. It is more than the soil and minerals, the sunlight and water that compose it. In one Oxford churchyard there stands a tree that was young at the time of King Arthur, and may survive until his return. For 1500 years it has dwelt there, maybe the oldest living thing in Oxford.

In 'Leaf by Niggle' Tolkien uses the metaphor of the tree in a way that affords us a rare glimpse into the way he understood his own art, and its importance for his life. The story is a kind of extended parable or allegory. Tolkien tells us in his Introductory Note that he woke up one morning with the whole story clear in his mind, and wrote it in haste. This was around 1939, when Tolkien (he tells us) was beginning to despair of ever finding out what had become of Gandalf or who Strider was. The hobbits had arrived at Bree: it was uncertain whether he would ever get them further. The carping of his academic colleagues, critical of him for wasting his energy on fairy-tales, must have been echoing loudly in his ears. War was looming.

The story concerns an amateur painter called Niggle, neighbour to a man called Parish. Niggle is working on a great painting: a huge tree set against a mountainous landscape. It began, Tolkien tells us, with an attempt to paint a single leaf caught in the wind. Niggle, of course, represents the author: his name reveals the earthly, day-to-day nature of artistic work. The 'leaf in the wind' might be the fragment of Anglo-Saxon poetry that we have already encountered. Tolkien must often have felt that his whole life was being frittered away on small textual details when the whole vista of the Silmarillion, for so long looming ever vaster in his mind, remained to be expressed. (Readers of 'The History of Middle-Earth' will be well aware just how much niggling Tolkien actually did!)

Mr Parish next door, of course, represents all those people who make demands on the artist's time, and take him away from what he feels he *ought* to be doing. As a Christian, Tolkien viewed every such person as a representative of Christ, a member of Christ's 'flock', and accepted the responsibility laid upon him by the Gospel to 'love your neighbour as yourself'. But most of Parish's demands appear at the time to be trivial, not least the exaggerated claim to illness which leads to Niggle himself catching cold and dying before his work is nearly completed.

Tolkien is presenting a humorous self-portrait here, and one that we can all identify with to some extent. Many of us have delusions of self-importance, and by contrast view the needs of others as less weighty than our own, regarding at times even the common courtesies of small-talk and social chit-chat as a tedious burden. The artist, driven and on fire with his inspiration, is liable to be even worse in this respect than most.

Much of the story is a description, in allegorical terms, of the after-death state known as Purgatory. Since this Catholic doctrine became something of a bone of contention during the Reformation, it is worth remarking that Tolkien's picture of it here is quite sensible and appealing. In fact it is clearly a kind of healing process. Exactly how long it takes is mysterious, since after death the normal measures of time are not applicable. It might well be said to take place in the very moment of dying. Tolkien describes Niggle as being placed in the 'Workhouse' for a century or so – clearly a bit of a joke against the popular notion of 'time in purgatory', which as a well-informed Catholic he knew to be false. Nor is the point of the Workhouse to punish Niggle, but rather to teach him to do 'one thing at a time' until he feels 'quieter inside'.

There follows an examination of his conscience by the Holy Trinity (three mysterious Voices overheard in the dark). Niggle's fundamental good will, despite all the imperfections of his bad temper and grudging, resentful attitude, is what finally counts in his favour. In Catholic teaching, Purgatory is the state of those who have been judged worthy of heaven, but 'only as through fire' (1 Cor. 3:15). The judgment of the soul has already taken place, though in the story Niggle is only ready to overhear the judgment when his purification is virtually complete.

Now his perception of the world has been washed clean, he is able to see all things as coming straight from the hands of God, as a 'gift'. He is sent off into the sunlight on a special train, arriving in an unexpected place: the very landscape he had been trying to paint. The Tree has been perfected, for it turns out the important thing on earth was not the accomplishment of the artist, which is always doomed to frustration, but the *intention*, which will be fulfilled in heaven. Furthermore the best parts of the Tree were not those which he had painted without interruption, but those in which his relationship to his neighbour Mr Parish had played a part.

2

A VERY GREAT STORY

Well, there you are: a hobbit amongst the Urukhai. Keep up
your hobbitry in heart, and think that *all* stories feel like that
when you are *in* them. You are inside a very great story!

J. R. R. Tolkien to his son Christopher
during the Second World War (L 66)

Twenty thousand Allied soldiers died on the first day of fighting in
the Battle of the Somme. To prevent his feelings from 'festering',
Tolkien began to write:

in grimy canteens, at lectures in cold fogs, in huts full of blas-
phemy and smut, or by candle light in bell-tents, even some
down in dugouts under shell fire. It did not make for
efficiency and present-mindedness, of course, and I was not a
good officer. . . (L 66).

The Lancashire Fusiliers won a record number of Victoria Crosses
for acts of bravery in that campaign. Tolkien won no medals, but he
had come to know and respect the heroes of the first 'modern' war:
ordinary Tommies who fought and died in the mud with all the
indomitable humour and dogged courage of hobbits. 'My "Sam
Gamgee" is indeed a reflection of the English soldier,' he wrote, 'of
the privates and batmen I knew in the 1914 war, and recognized as

so far superior to myself.'³ *The Lord of the Rings* was an exploration of English heroism in the wars that laid the foundations of the modern world.

THE HOBBIT: THERE AND BACK AGAIN

Even so, *The Lord of the Rings* could not have been written in 1917. Tolkien may have met Sam, but Sam was not yet a 'hobbit'. The magic word emerged spontaneously in an idle moment during the early 1930s, while Tolkien was marking some student essays and came across a blank page. 'In a hole in the ground there lived a hobbit,' he doodled – and then began to wonder what the word meant.

Hobbits turned out to be two to four feet tall, a 'merry folk' who dressed in bright colours and seldom wore shoes because their feet 'had tough leathery soles and were clad in thick curling hair'. Little interested in machinery more complicated than a water-mill (though they possessed clocks, umbrellas and fireworks), they were a settled, unadventurous, agrarian people, an affectionate caricature of the rural English whom Tolkien knew as a child.

By 1930 Tolkien was writing a story for children that became *The Hobbit*. It was this that established his popularity as a writer when it was published seven years later. The hobbit of the title, Bilbo Baggins, is plucked from his sedate existence at Bag End in Hobbiton by the wizard Gandalf, who appears before his round, green door when Bilbo is around fifty years old (young for a hobbit) and arranges for him to accompany the dwarf Thorin Oakenshield and his companions in a quest to regain lost treasure from a dragon called Smaug. What begins as a comedy gradually becomes more serious, as Bilbo discovers his courage and saves the dwarves from various perils, finally becoming, if not a dragon-slayer then at least a burglar of the dragon's lair and eventually an effective diplomat. In the Battle of Five Armies, representing Orcs (goblins) and Wolves, Men, Elves and Dwarves, Bilbo is caught up in the great events of Middle-earth.

The key stylistic innovation which appears in this book and became the foundation for *The Lord of the Rings* reflects a fundamental tension in Tolkien's imagination. On the one hand he was writing this story for his children. On the other, the mythology, the Silmarillion that had begun to take shape in his notebooks since the war, was pulling the narrative towards a very different genre of writing: archaic, poetic, high-flown, epic. The result was what C. S. Lewis describes as a 'shift in tone' within *The Hobbit* itself, a change in the style of the language sufficient to carry the reader almost without realising it from an every-day world a modern child can identify with into the universe of mythology, romance and chivalry, and back again.

The shift in tone from humdrum and comic to high epic is reflected in the voice of the narrator, who at the beginning of the book is telling us 'He had a horrible thought that the cakes might run short, and then he – as the host: he knew his duty and stuck to it how-ever painful – he might have to go without,' by the end of the story, after the death of the dragon, is saying such things as: 'Many took ill of wet and cold and sorrow that night, and afterwards died, who had escaped uninjured from the ruin of the town; and in the days that fol-lowed there was much sickness and great hunger.' The tone adopted by the narrator – by turns patronising, pompous and cruel – is one of the interesting features of the book. In *Tolkien's Art* (a book about Tolkien's multi-layered craftsmanship) Jane Chance argues that the *persona* of the narrator is a deliberate literary construction by the author, intended as a satire on the literary critics he despised.

In the face of all this complexity of style, Bilbo's speech patterns remain constant. 'Really you know, things are impossible. Personally I am tired of the whole affair. I wish I was back in the West in my own home, where folk are more reasonable.' Constant, that is, until the death of Thorin, where the two worlds truly come together in what is a scene of reconciliation on many levels:

> Farewell, King under the Mountain! This is a bitter adven-ture, if it must end so; and not a mountain of gold can amend

it. Yet I am glad that I have shared in your perils – that has been more than any Baggins deserves.

Bilbo's acquisition of a magic ring under the Misty Mountains – a ring that makes the wearer invisible – corresponds to a growth in his own inner confidence, as he learns independence of mind and begins to use his own gifts and talents. Dangerous adventures alternating with moments of respite – usually involving food – provide him with a series of initiations. The journey begins and ends at Bag End, and in both cases with an unexpected tea party. But (as Jane Chance has also pointed out) Bilbo's attitude to his guests has changed, marking his growth from selfish squire to generous host, welcoming his guests with joy, and in his final words 'thanking goodness' for being, as Gandalf says, 'quite a little fellow in a wide world after all'.

Bilbo is a hero virtually inconceivable in an earlier era (except as comic relief, perhaps), able to assume a central role in the narrative despite his apparently peripheral involvement in the great events of dragon-slaying and battle. Tolkien renders the heroic motives of Thorin and the others all too transparent, and we see the pride and selfishness that lies behind them as the dwarf reclaims his kingdom and refuses to share his new-found wealth with those of other races who brought about the victory. Yet we see deeper still, to the goodness that lies beneath and which emerges in the form of repentance as Thorin lies on his deathbed.

THE LORD OF THE RINGS

The Hobbit was an unexpected success and Tolkien's publishers wanted a sequel. Of course, what he wanted to offer them was the Silmarillion, but they demanded 'more hobbits', and this meant that he had to start again with the little people: Bilbo, Frodo, Sam, Merry and Pippin. Thus providentially what we end up with in the new book is not a chronicle of mythological wars, but another journey 'there and back again' from the mundane to the epic, the everyday to the heroic and back to the mundane. Even more than in the shorter book, this was a literary bridge that proved effective in carrying traffic in both directions. It transposes the hobbits into an epic universe, and through them it brings the epic qualities of nobility and courage into the world of the Shire.

In developing his sequel, Tolkien reworked the first version of *The Hobbit* to make it more clearly an episode in the wider history of Middle-earth, a branch on the tree of his Silmarillion. The finding of the Ring under the Misty Mountains became now the centre of the story, from having been an 'accident along the way'. It is revealed as something long sought by the Enemy: the One Ring cut from his hand at the end of the Second Age, and now needed to restore his full power. Bilbo's earlier account of the finding of the Ring, revised in later editions of *The Hobbit*, was explained in the Prologue of the longer work as evidence that the Ring itself had begun quickly to work on his mind and heart, as it had long before upon Gollum, being inhabited by a part of its Master's evil spirit. The new book was therefore painted on a much vaster canvas, with a much greater range of colours, many of them unexpectedly dark, and some piercingly bright.

The new story employed the same simple structure as *The Hobbit* to provide the backbone of the plot: a journey into the wild, consisting of a series of light and dark moments, brushes with death alternating with respite in the 'homely houses' of Butterbur, Bombadil, Elrond, Galadriel and Faramir. The goal of the quest is not to retrieve a treasure but to lose one: the Ring must be 'unmade' in the fire of its forging, cast into Mount Doom under the very eye of the Dark Lord. If it fails and the Ring returns to its maker, his power to rule will be vastly increased. Elves and men once successfully opposed him, but an age has passed and the free peoples have become depleted and divided. The existence of the Ring, even outside Sauron's possession, poses the main threat; whereas if it is destroyed, the link binding the Dark Lord's armies and even his own physical substance will be dissolved. Bilbo's heir, Frodo, volunteers to carry the Ring to Mordor:

> An overwhelming longing to rest and remain at peace by Bilbo's side in Rivendell filled all his heart. At last with an effort he spoke, and wondered to hear his own words, as if some other will was using his small voice.
>
> 'I will take the Ring,' he said, 'though I do not know the way.'

(It may *feel* like another's will, but that it is truly his own is implied by the fact that he speaks with an effort, against the pressure of a selfish desire. Yet Tolkien's 'as if' does carry some weight: in key passages this phrase usually means more than it says. There is another will involved here, but it is a will that does not force or dominate, a will that strengthens our own when we try to do the right thing.)

Frodo is supported along the way by a fellowship of eight companions chosen in Rivendell. The Hobbits are represented by Sam, Merry and Pippin. Men are represented by Boromir and the ranger Aragorn, the latter now revealed as the heir to the long-vacant throne of Gondor. Legolas for the Elves, Gimli for the Dwarves and Gandalf complete the Nine. Tolkien gives each of these major protagonists a story of his own, interwoven with the others in a complicated, almost musical harmony that converges on a double climax as the quest is achieved. There is a tenth strand, too, which pulls the whole together, and it is the story of Gollum, the Ring's previous owner (or victim), who pursues it to the very end.

Quite why the Ring cannot simply be transported to Mount Doom by friendly eagles is never explained, but it is strongly implied that the task is one that can only be achieved in this, the hard way. The Ring is a spiritual force that must be carried by the weakest and humblest of creatures, and one to whom the task has been 'appointed' by providence. Naturally, the plan appears as nothing less than folly to the worldly-wise, and this is precisely the reason it is finally adopted.

As Gandalf says, 'let folly be our cloak, a veil before the eyes of the Enemy! For he is very wise, and weighs all things to a nicety in the scales of his malice.' The Enemy cannot suspect that those who hold the Ring will refuse to use it, and even seek to destroy it.

Already the Christian ethos of the book has become apparent:

> For God's foolishness is wiser than human wisdom, and God's weakness is stronger than human strength . . . God chose what is foolish in the world to shame the wise; God chose what is weak in the world to shame the strong; God chose what is low and despised in the world, things that are not, to reduce to nothing things that are (1 Cor. 1:25, 27–8).

In fact, as the adventure proceeds, Frodo emerges as a very 'Christian' type of hero. For Christians the true hero is not the one who succeeds in imposing his own will on others by virtue of outward, physical strength, or even by the inner strength that comes from intelligence and moderation of appetite. He allows himself to be humiliated and crucified. He refuses earthly respect and glory for the sake of something much greater: not merely his own integrity, but the will of the Father in heaven; not for the self, in other words, but for the transcendent Other, for God and for neighbour. In Frodo's case, he does what he knows he must for the sake of others: 'I tried to save the Shire, and it has been saved, but not for me.'

Christianity does not simply deny the traditional heroic virtues, but transforms them, raising them to a higher level. Saint Paul is therefore able to emphasise the heroic qualities of Christ almost as though he were describing a traditional military chieftain (Col. 1:20; 2:15). But what is defeated by this hero, what is wrestled to the ground and destroyed, is nothing less than death itself.

Furthermore, for Christianity, since every person is equally important in the eyes of God, *anyone and everyone* can be a hero. You do not have to be a member of the elite, or the warrior caste, nor just a representative of the people. The poor are raised up to the thrones of princes, the strong are humbled, and the rich are sent empty away. As Elrond says: 'This is the hour of the Shire-folk, when they arise from their quiet fields to shake the towers and counsels of the Great.'

The day Frodo and his companions set out on their mission in the depths of winter is given by Tolkien in the narrative as 25 December. The date serves Tolkien well, for it was a pagan festival long before it became a Christian one, but at the same time it signals to the Christian reader the fact that there is a connection between the mission of the Ring-bearer and that of Christ, who was sent out not from Rivendell but from his mother's womb on the same date.[4]

The mission of Frodo increasingly resembles that of Christ as the journey approaches its end. The slow passage of the Dead Marshes, surrounded by the faint lights and uncanny faces of the dead warriors, and of Shelob's Lair on the borders of Mordor where he falls to the ground, both recall the Garden of Gethsemane, not least because Frodo is betrayed to Shelob under cover of darkness by the companion he tried to save (Gollum). The long carrying of the Ring to Mount Doom, as it grows in weight and power, dragging him to the ground, resembles the way of the cross. The help that Sam gives him in bearing the burden reminds us of the man called Simon, dragooned by the soldiers into helping Jesus with his cross when it became too heavy for him.

The apocalyptic events that ensue are narrated in a way that inevitably recalls the Book of Revelation, from the rescue of Frodo and Sam from the slopes of the wrecked mountain by eagles (Rev. 12:14), to the token of Frodo's eventual transformation, the 'white gem like a star' he is given by Arwen when she offers him her place on the ship to the West. 'To everyone who conquers I will give some of the hidden manna, and I will give a white stone, and on the white stone is written a new name that no one knows except the one who receives it' (Rev. 2:17). The triumphant song of the eagle, 'Sing and be glad, all ye children of the West, for your king shall come again,' reminds us in mood and tone of the words of the seventh angel of the Apocalypse, 'The kingdom of the world has become the kingdom of

our Lord and of his Messiah, and he will reign for ever and ever'
(Rev. 11:15).

THE TRIUMPH OF MERCY

In all these ways, and in the persistent motif of death and resurrection, Tolkien's Christian genius reveals itself. Nowhere is the subtlety of this genius more visible than in a final twist of the plot within
the inner chamber of Mount Doom itself. This deserves some closer
attention, for it marks an important difference between Frodo and
Christ. Frodo is no mere allegorical stand-in, but a true character in
his own right. On the very brink of success, his free will having
taken him as far as it can, he renounces the quest and claims the Ring
for his own. It becomes clear that his ability to cast it away has been
eroded by the task of bearing it so far. His assertion of ownership
over the Ring signifies the loss of his self-possession, and the words
he uses betray this: he says, 'I do not choose now to do what I came
to do. I will not do this deed. The Ring is mine.'

Note that he does not say, 'I choose . . . I do', but rather 'I do not
choose . . . I will not do'. Behind this choice of words lies a great
weight of tradition – indeed, a whole theory of ethics. The Christian
reader may discern an echo of St Paul's words: 'I can will what is
right, but I cannot do it' (Rom. 7:18–19). What is being suggested is
that ethics, or right behaviour, hinges on *what we have the power to
do*. Frodo sees himself as choosing – choosing to claim the Ring. But
in fact he has lost the power not to claim it. Christian ethics is about
attaining freedom, which does not mean the freedom to do whatever
we want but rather the *power to do the right thing*.

Tolkien wrote of Frodo's failure that it reflected the fact that the
power of Evil in the world cannot, in the end, be defeated by us
on our own, however 'good' we may try to be (L 191). By implicitly denying the heresy of Pelagianism (the idea that we can
become good entirely by our own power), Tolkien is simply being
realistic about our situation in a fallen world. This is not pes-

simism, however; for while we cannot save ourselves, *we can yet be saved.*

A reader quotes St Paul's remark (1 Cor. 10:13) that God 'will not let you be tested beyond your strength, but with the testing he will also provide the way out so that you may be able to endure it', but Tolkien responds to this by evoking the cases, so familiar in the modern world, of prisoners issuing from captivity broken and insane, perhaps brainwashed by their captors, where no such immediate deliverance by God was available. Such people should be judged by their original intentions, not by their moral 'failure' under intolerable torment. In relation to Frodo, he writes (in L 191) that a more appropriate Bible passage would be those familiar lines from the Lord's Prayer: 'Lead us not into temptation, but deliver us from evil.'

For God *does* seem to permit us to be placed in positions beyond our power, and in those cases the 'way out' to which St Paul refers will depend on the previous exercise of virtues such as mercy or humility, which will already have created the circumstances for salvation, if not of physical escape. Once again, Tolkien affirms that he did not impose his own solution on the story: it emerged from the characters themselves, and followed from the logic of their decisions. Thus, Frodo deserved all the honour he received on the Field of Cormallen. He had spent himself completely in the service of his mission. The sacrifices he had made had brought him to the destined point. Perhaps no one else could have got even as far as that (L 192).

And so, when Gollum bites the Ring from Frodo's finger and falls into the Fire, this is the consequence of Frodo's earlier (and freer) decision to spare Gollum's life. The salvation of the world, and of Frodo himself, is brought about in consequence of the pity and forgiveness that he had shown to Gollum earlier in the story (L 181). Thus in the end it is not Frodo who saves Middle-earth at all, though he bore the Ring to the Mountain, nor Gollum, who took the Ring into the Fire. It can only be God himself, working through the love and freedom of his creatures, using even our mistakes and the designs of the Enemy (as *The Silmarillion* hints that he will do) to bring about our good. The scene is a triumph of providence over fate, but also a triumph of mercy, in which free will, supported by grace, is fully vindicated.

And what of Gollum? Even he is no cipher, no allegory or shadow only, but a fully three-dimensional character (beautifully realised, it has to be said, in the Peter Jackson movie). We are meant to pity as well as fear Gollum, and we do. We learn of his long existence as a slave of the Ring, which feeds on his petty desires, jealousies and resentments, magnifying them into an artificial substitute for life, indefinitely prolonged. We know that he has committed evil deeds beyond count, yet we are shown the conflict that still torments him as the mercy shown by Frodo eats away at the foundations of his malice. One of the most moving scenes in the book, which caused Tolkien to weep as he wrote it, takes place on the stairs of Cirith Ungol as Gollum comes back to find Frodo and Sam lying asleep, Frodo's head in Sam's lap, and peace in both their faces.

He reaches out a trembling hand to touch Frodo very gently.

> For a fleeting moment, could one of the sleepers have seen him, they would have thought that they beheld an old weary hobbit, shrunken by the years that had carried him far beyond his time, beyond friends and kin, and the fields and streams of youth, an old starved pitiable thing.

But Sam wakes to see him, as he thinks, 'pawing at Master' and shouts at him roughly. The fleeting moment of grace passes beyond recall. Gollum's resolve to betray them is renewed, and he falls into the Fire still enslaved.

In Letter 181 Tolkien muses on the fate of Gollum, and the subtlety of his moral vision becomes evident. Sméagol was broken by the Ring, but he would never have acquired it in the first place if he had not already made himself a thief and a potential murderer of his own brother. Yet his will was still not totally corrupted many centuries later.

By temporising, not fixing the still not wholly corrupt Sméagol-will towards good in the debate in the slag hole, he weakened himself for the final chance when dawning love of Frodo was too easily withered by the jealousy of Sam before Shelob's lair.

He weakened himself, Tolkien says. Few writers are as conscious as this of the moral responsibility we each bear for our own fate. Tolkien allows his characters to make their own decisions for good or evil. Yet even so he does not judge them, for (as he adds) 'we who are "in the same boat" must not usurp the Judge.'

THE RETURN OF THE KING

The immediate result of the Ring's destruction is the fall of the Dark Tower. In some very real sense, the Ring was the foundation on which the tower of Barad-dûr was built. Now its 'towers and battle-ments, tall as hills . . . great courts and dungeons, eyeless prisons sheer as cliffs, and gaping gates of steel and adamant' crumble and slide into the ruin of Mordor. All the paraphernalia of oppression, of politics for the sake of power, hang on one thing and one thing only: the thing symbolised by the Ring, now consumed by the Fire.

The victory of the allies follows swiftly. Their enemies are demor-alised, scattered and witless. Aragorn is merciful and wise in judge-ment, and enters the city of Gondor with a healing hand. His coronation is itself an act of healing for the whole kingdom, bring-ing to an end the long sickness of Gondor and Arnor, the shadow of the Shadow upon men.

Aragorn, the grim-visaged ranger of the wilderness who becomes King Elessar, is of course a type of King Arthur, and Gandalf a type of Merlin. In Aragorn, as in Arthur, the royal blood has to prove itself worthy of kingship by heroism. Arthur pulls the sword from the stone and founds the kingdom of Logres. Aragorn reforges 'the sword that was broken', and reunites the two halves of the kingdom appointed to him, inaugurating a new age of the world. Merlin and Gandalf both function here as the representatives of Tradition, of the wisdom of the past – of memory, you might say. Both of them depart the kingdom once the legitimacy of the king has been established, the royal heritage transmitted.

Did Tolkien mean to suggest that Aragorn is the distant ancestor of Arthur? In Chapter IX of Book V of *The Lord of the Rings*, Legolas mentions a prophecy that Lúthien's line will never fail. It seems possible. If these stories were originally intended as a mythology for England, it might have made sense to create an Elvish ancestry for the greatest king of Christian legend.

But the more important point is that in the story of King Elessar, and the other interwoven 'kingly' motifs in the book, Tolkien is revealing profound truths about the royal authority that each of us must reinstate at the centre of our own inner kingdoms, and the moral virtues of courtesy, courage and chivalry that underpin that authority. Aragorn is a true king not only because of his lineage and the tokens of kingship he bears, but because he turns *back* from his royal quest to help the hobbits, because of his years of selfless service as a ranger, because of his faithfulness to Arwen.

The King who is borne up by the tacit assent of his people, in whom all recognise the principle of justice tempered with mercy, whose authority flows from his humility before truth, is no doubt a rare man. *The Lord of the Rings* presents us with his portrait, an ideal portrait and thereby a guide to the pure principle of royalty. (See pp. 126–9.) But the true King exists in the real world, as Tolkien knew. All the prophecies, all the types and shadows, Aragorn as well as Arthur, converge on Christ, king of a realm as wide as creation.

Aragorn rides the Paths of the Dead, and frees the ghostly army of Oathbreakers from their curse by enlisting them against the darkness. At the Black Stone of Erech he unveils the standard of his realm that no man living can see, for it is night; but the living dead sense it, and follow. Jesus, of whom Aragorn is but a type or prefigurement in Tolkien's mythical history, enlists us in the 'war of the Logos' by unveiling the standard of his own kingdom in the darkness of the Passion. Those who are spiritually dead, though they still walk the earth awaiting the fulfilment of prophecy, may recognise the love of God that reveals itself by descending; and follow it through death into a new day rising.

> On the throne sat a mail-clad man, a great sword was laid across his knees, but he wore no helm. As they drew near he rose. And then they knew him, changed as he was, so high and glad of face, kingly, lord of Men, dark-haired with eyes of grey.
>
> Frodo ran to meet him, and Sam followed close behind, 'Well, if that isn't the crown of all!' he said. 'Strider, or I'm still asleep!'

We too need the King to take his throne, in his 'great stone castle away down south'. For then we can go back to our own polluted landscape, with its mean brick houses and its small-minded officials, its devastated orchards and avenues of trees. We can return there endowed with the authority of servants and friends of the King, to commence our own task: the task which awaits us at home.

THE SCOURING OF THE SHIRE

The great battles are over, the Ring of Power destroyed, and the King restored to the ancient throne of Gondor. Frodo and Sam have been honoured on the field of Cormallen for accomplishing the quest. The hobbits, transformed and ennobled, return to the Shire and must now defeat the unexpected evil that they find there.

> The Old Grange on the west side had been knocked down, and its place taken by rows of tarred sheds. All the chestnuts were gone. The banks and hedgerows were broken. Great wagons were standing in disorder in a field beaten bare of grass. Bagshot Row was a yawning sand and gravel quarry.

Bag End up beyond could not be seen for a clutter of large huts.

The returning hobbits find their beloved homeland despoiled, polluted and enslaved. The people of the Shire are now working for men who bully and exploit them, imprisoning any who break the numerous new rules and regulations. They are forced to live in poverty and fear, while the ruffians eat, drink and smoke the fruit of the land. Traditional hobbit-holes are being replaced with ugly brick houses. In other words, the hobbits returned expecting to find again their secure, happy, rural community, and instead have come face to face with the industrial squalor of post-war England.

It is the exiled wizard Saruman who turns out to be responsible for all this, in a final act of revenge against the hobbits who brought about the destruction of Orthanc. His headquarters in the Shire, and thus the centre of the evil infection, is Bag End itself, Bilbo's, Frodo's and (eventually) Sam's home, the heart of Tolkien's interior world.

The success of the hobbits in dealing with this final peril would not have been possible – would certainly not have been believable – if they had not experienced the epic adventure as a whole, and if we had not seen them transformed into heroes of song and legend; so that when they are plunged back into the banality of the Shire they are able to defeat the evil that they find with the grace – the gifts – that they have received in their travels. Those hobbits who have not been so initiated into heroism are helpless to oppose a force that enslaves by fear and the exploitation of self-interest. But the travellers have passed through darkness, in the Barrows, in Moria, in battle and in Mordor itself. The half-darkness of everyday evil holds no terrors for them. They have been broken and re-forged through service to others: to Frodo, to Théoden, to Denethor, to the peoples of Middle-earth.

Merry and Pippin, indeed, have been prepared in a special way for the task that now lies before them. Merry has been taken into

Théoden's service, ridden with the Mark to aid Gondor, and aided Eowyn in the destruction of the Ringwraith whose breath causes despair. Merry's special gift, then, is the overcoming of despair and the raising of hope – signified by the ancient Horn of the Mark which is given to him by Éomer at their parting. Pippin has served Denethor the Steward of Gondor, Théoden's darkened image, learning to obey but also to transcend obedience when a higher good requires rules to be broken: in this case he is able to save Faramir whom Denethor has ordered to be burned while still alive.

When they return to the Shire it is Pippin who will tear up the 'Rules' imposed by Saruman's men, and which the hobbits have passively accepted; while it is Merry who raises their hearts with the Horn of Rohan. Both of them have been prepared, also, by the direct assault on Saruman's Orthanc with the Ents: a rising of nature herself against the 'mind of metal and wheels', as Treebeard calls him.

The biblical Book of Wisdom tells us: 'the creation, serving you who made it, exerts itself to punish the unrighteous' (16:24). Saruman, trembling in his tower, illustrates the truth of these words.

> For not even the inner chamber that held them protected them from fear, but terrifying sounds rang out around them, and dismal phantoms with gloomy faces appeared . . . The delusions of their magic art lay humbled, and their boasted wisdom was scornfully rebuked (17:4, 7).

As the hobbits arrive in the Shire they meet one of Saruman's men. At Frodo's words, 'The King's messengers will ride up the Greenway now, not bullies from Isengard,' he merely sneers. This is too much for Pippin.

> 'I am a messenger of the King,' he said. 'You are speaking to the King's friend, and one of the most renowned in all the lands of the West. You are a ruffian and a fool. Down on your knees in the road and ask pardon, or I will set this troll's bane in you!'

[43]

The scouring of the Shire is written not just as an account of the author's psychological and spiritual journey, but as a call to arms to the reader, as a blast on the Horn of Rohan summoning us to the help of our friends and the healing of our world. We too, if we have imaginatively accompanied the hobbits on this journey from the mundane to the epic and back again, are initiated into the realities that exist behind the veils of everyday life. Tolkien hints that a similar heroism is called for in us, as we see the England of our own day labouring under the disguised slavery of consumerism and overrun by half-orcs who despise our traditional way of life.

This is the heroism which expresses itself not by the sword (although strong action may indeed be called for), but by placing ourselves at the service of the Light in whatever way is demanded of us in our own circumstances. 'I do so dearly believe,' Tolkien wrote, 'that no half-heartedness and no worldly fear must turn us aside from following the light unflinchingly.'[5]

THE RİNG TODAY

Tolkien wrote a letter to his son Christopher in 1944. Referring to the news of his son's first solo flight with the RAF, so different from the silent skimming of the birds that men dreamed of attaining when they sought to fly, he remarks: 'There is the tragedy and despair of all machinery laid bare' (L 75).

Within *The Lord of the Rings*, Isengard under the wizard Saruman illustrates the 'tragedy and despair' of reliance on technology. In the modern world, we have seen the devastating and dehumanising effects of a purely pragmatic and quantitative approach to nature. The Romantic movement, from Blake and Coleridge to Barfield and Tolkien, believed there must be an alternative. Goethe even tried to lay the foundations for it: he called it a 'science of qualities'. At the end of his wonderful essay *The Abolition of Man*, C. S. Lewis writes of a 'regenerate science' of the future that 'would not do even to minerals and vegetables what modern science threatens to do to man himself. When it explained it would not explain away. When it spoke of the parts it would remember the whole.' And he adds:

> You cannot go on 'explaining away' for ever: you will find you have explained explanation itself away. You cannot go on 'seeing through' things for ever. The whole point of seeing through something is to see something through it. It is good that the window should be transparent, because the street or garden beyond it is opaque. How if you saw through the garden too? It is no use trying to 'see through' first principles. If you see through everything, then everything is transparent. But a wholly transparent world is an invisible world. To 'see through' all things is the same as not to see.'[6]

Lewis here echoes Tolkien's concern with technology. He compares Francis Bacon with Marlowe's Faustus. For modern science and black magic alike the goal was power. Magic and superstition gave way before science mainly for pragmatic reasons: it proved to be more effective. But the 'magician's bargain' tells us the price of such power over the forces of nature: our own souls. For, says Lewis,

> if man chooses to treat himself as raw material, raw material he will be: not raw material to be manipulated, as he fondly imagined, by himself, but by mere appetite, that is, mere Nature, in the person of his de-humanized Conditioners.

The conquest of nature turns out to be our conquest *by* nature, that is to say by our own desires or those of others; and the Master becomes, in the end, a puppet.

In Letter 131 Tolkien contrasts the 'magic' (technology) of the Elves with that of the Enemy: the goal of the former is Art, whereas the aim of the latter is 'domination and tyrannous re-forming of Creation'. The devices of the Elves are benign. They work with the grain of nature, not against it. Tolkien is not opposed to technology *per se*, but to the kind of technology that issues from a certain mentality of control. The desire for power, he writes, 'leads to the

Machine (or Magic)': the use of our talents or devices to bulldoze other wills.

The Ring of Power, the 'One Ring to bring them all and in the darkness bind them', is a symbol or example of this kind of technology: the ultimate machine. In making devices like the Ring to increase our domination of others, we inevitably make ourselves weaker by becoming dependent on them (L 211). They magnify our power but also externalise it, so that we ourselves wither by their use. When they are destroyed, that weakness is exposed. Sauron, when the Ring is destroyed, literally blows away on the wind.

The search for worldly control – power over nature and over others, which is to say 'technological' and 'psychological' power – is in the end self-defeating. The only true power is spiritual, and is exercised primarily over oneself. The ruler who first rules himself is also able genuinely to represent his people. He is not a man alone, but a man loved and supported by others. If he does not impose his own will upon his subordinates and thereby dissipate it, the will of his subordinates will flourish and support him. King Elessar is such a ruler. In the long run, a society built on respect and mutual support is always going to be stronger than a pseudo-society built on fear and self-interest.

Tolkien's most developed reflections on the nature of evil and the corruption of power can be found in *Morgoth's Ring*. Sauron may be the Dark Lord of the Third Age, but once he had been merely the servant and lieutenant of a much more powerful entity, Melkor, known to the Elves as Morgoth. Expelled from the world at the end of the First Age, Morgoth's shadow still lies across Middle-earth. In the section 'Myths Transformed', Tolkien reflects on the similarities and differences between these two figures.

Both make themselves vulnerable, ultimately, by seeking dominion. Morgoth acts through agents that he seeks always to control: armies, orcs, balrogs. For the sake of efficiency these must be made capable of acting to some extent on his behalf without having specific orders. Tolkien writes: 'Part of his native creative power has gone out into making an independent evil growth out of his control.' Sauron's weakness was due to the fact that he had placed a large part of his power into the Ring. But the power of Morgoth, originally much greater, has also gone out into a 'Ring'. Morgoth's Ring, Tolkien tells us, is the whole of Middle-earth, and his power runs even through the physical elements of which it is composed – including gold, apparently, more than silver. Water is one of the few elements that is almost entirely outside Morgoth's influence.

This explains the basis for the evil magic practised by Sauron, for he is able to work with the 'Morgoth-ingredient' in things, such as fire and gold in the case of the Rings of Power. It also helps to explain the general 'taintedness' of Middle-earth (outside Lothlórien, which is specially protected). It explains the fact that nature is subject to disease and corruption, perhaps even to entropy, and it explains the world-weariness of the Elves, which is due not to their longevity so much as to the 'tendency towards Melkor' inherent in earthly matter, including the matter of their bodies while in Middle-earth.

> Morgoth lost (or exchanged, or transmuted) the greater part of his original 'angelic' powers, of mind and spirit, while gaining a terrible grip upon the physical world . . . Sauron's, relatively smaller, power was *concentrated*; Morgoth's vast power was *disseminated*.

In 'Myths Transformed' Tolkien also explains that whereas Morgoth's motivations are almost purely nihilistic, Sauron (very like the corrupt Saruman later on in the history) had no objection to the existence of the world as such, as long as it was under his control:

> He still had the relics of positive purposes, that descended from the good of the nature in which he began: it had been his virtue (and therefore also the cause of his fall, and of his relapse) that he loved order and co-ordination, and disliked all confusion and wasteful friction.

The empire of Sauron, then, is on a different scale, on a different order, from that of Morgoth, though by the concentration of his power Sauron becomes for a while stronger than Morgoth in his later 'dissipated' phase. It is an empire that depends not only on slaves such as orcs, but also on willing human vassals (Easterlings and others) who, for their own perceived advantage, or out of fear of reprisals, pay tribute to Mordor and even send armies to fight for Sauron when summoned to do so. Such arrangements are not uncommon among the 'evil empires' of today.

How, then, should we treat such an enemy? Tolkien was always conscious of the temptation that besets the righteous: to employ an evil means in a good cause. This was how the great had fallen, how Gandalf and Galadriel might have fallen, and how we ourselves can still fall. The Easterlings are redeemable. What of Orcs, who were not made but only bred and corrupted by Morgoth? In 'Myths Transformed' there is an interesting note. The Orcs, Tolkien writes:

> might have become irredeemable (at least by Elves and Men), but they remained within the Law. That is, that though of necessity, being the fingers of the hand of Morgoth, they must be fought with the utmost severity, they must not be dealt with in their own terms of cruelty and treachery. Captives must not be tormented, not even to discover information for the defence of the homes of Elves and Men. If any Orcs surrendered and asked for mercy, they must be granted it, even at a cost. This was the teaching of the Wise, though in the horror of the War it was not always heeded.

Tolkien always insisted that his fantasy was not an allegory. Mordor was not Nazi Germany, or Soviet Russia, any more than it was intended to be Saddam's Iraq. 'To ask if the Orcs "are" Communists is to me as sensible as asking if Communists are Orcs' (L 203). But at the same time he did not deny that the story was 'applicable' to contemporary affairs, indeed he affirmed this. It is applicable not merely in providing a parable to illustrate the danger of the machine, but in showing the reasons for that danger: sloth and stupidity, pride, greed, folly and lust for power, all exemplified in the various races of Middle-earth (see L 203).

Against these vices he set courage and courtesy, kindness and humility, generosity and wisdom, in those same hearts. There is a universal moral law, but it is not the law of a tyrant. It is the law that makes it possible for us to be free.

The world Tolkien describes is our own, though he does so in the mode of fantasy, and the 'very great story' he tells us is one that continues in our own day.

3

A HIDDEN PRESENCE: TOLKIEN'S CATHOLICISM

A letter to his friend Robert Murray SJ in December 1953 contains Tolkien's famous comment:

> *The Lord of the Rings* is of course a fundamentally religious and Catholic work; unconsciously so at first, but consciously in the revision. That is why I have not put in, or have cut out, practically all references to anything like 'religion', to cults or practices, in the imaginary world. For the religious element is absorbed into the story and the symbolism (L 142).

He goes on to say that this 'sounds more self-important than I feel', for he has 'consciously planned very little'.

The Lord of the Rings is nevertheless Christian and orthodox in intention and spirit. It is permeated with a sense of eternity, of the objective order of good and evil, and of an all-wise providence (the sense that God somehow orders all things, even apparent coincidences): this is all part of that 'forgotten sunlight' which serves to awaken us from the sleep of materialism. The spirit of courtesy that we see in Aragorn and Faramir, the respect for women and the determination to protect the weak, the virtues of courage and fortitude and prudence and justice that shine in these noble characters, are patterns of goodness that were learned from the Gospel.

Tolkien saw in the Christian revelation the meeting and fusing of legend and history, and in the Body of Christ the restored bridge from this world to the other. He persuaded C. S. Lewis of this (though Chesterton's *Everlasting Man* was already an influence) during a walk in the grounds of Magdalen College, celebrated in Tolkien's long poem *Mythopoeia*. He turned on its head the old rationalist argument against Christianity – that it was 'too good to be true', and must consequently be dismissed as a kind of wishful thinking. What if we wish it to be true because that desire has been planted in our nature by the One who made us? After all, the phenomenon of hunger proves the existence of food. Myths of a dying god resurrected, or fairy-tales of healing and of virtue vindicated, exist because we cannot help seeking what we were made to find. Nature was made for grace. Our hearts spoke true, and in Jesus Christ the Author of the world has once and for all vindicated those fleeting glimpses of 'Joy beyond the walls of the world, poignant as grief,' which art affords us.

Clearly Tolkien did not see himself as a religious writer in the same sense as Lewis. He did not feel called to enter the lists as a writer on Christian themes, let alone as a theologian or philosopher of religion. Nevertheless, with the posthumous publication in 1981 of his *Letters*, this side of his life was exposed to view, and it became clear the Catholic belief and sensibility he received from his mother and later from his guardian, Father Morgan, whom he called a 'second father', permeated every aspect of his life.

The American Catholic Flannery O' Connor also wrote in a way that is not explicitly 'religious'. Like Tolkien, she wanted to portray the way grace and sin operate in the real world:

> This all means that what we roughly call the Catholic novel is not necessarily about a Christianized or Catholicized world, but simply that it is one in which the truth as Christians know it has been used as a light to see the world by . . . The novelist is required to create the illusion of a

whole world with believable people in it, and the chief difference between the novelist who is an orthodox Christian and the novelist who is merely a naturalist is that the Christian novelist lives in a larger universe. He believes that the natural world contains the supernatural. And this doesn't mean that his obligation to portray the natural is less; it means it is greater.[7]

Flannery O'Connor had no desire to build alternative cosmologies on Tolkien's grand scale, but what she says about her own artistry applies as well to him as to herself. I am not claiming to judge Tolkien's degree of sanctity, but I do think he had what we call today a 'spirituality', and that it shines through his writing. To a puzzled non-Christian, who tells him that he has created a world 'in which some sort of faith seems to be everywhere without a visible source, like light from an invisible lamp' (L 328), Tolkien replies:

> Of his own sanity no man can securely judge. If sanctity inhabits his work or as a pervading light illumines it then it does not come from him but through him. And neither of you would perceive it in these terms unless it was with you also. Otherwise you would see and feel nothing, or (if some other spirit was present) you would be filled with contempt, nausea, hatred. 'Leaves out of the elf-country, gah! Lembas — dust and ashes, we don't eat that.'

THE ORDER OF GRACE

Tolkien's spirituality was, of course, deeply Catholic. And the first thing to note is that the specifically *Catholic* dimension of Christianity is almost entirely bound up with the Blessed Virgin Mary. The dogmas about Mary bring to a focus or 'enshrine', if you like, everything that Catholics believe about the Incarnation and human destiny, about God's love for his creation and the way he intends to save it from death.

By giving Mary the title *Theotokos* (literally 'god-bearer'), the early Church at the Council of Ephesus was not trying to elevate a mere creature above the eternal God, as though Mary had existed before God himself. The title was designed to contradict a popular heresy, to the effect that Jesus had been merely a human person, and only later (at the moment of his baptism in the Jordan) came to be inhabited by a divine spirit. What the Church wanted to say was that Jesus all along was a human being but not a human *person.*

The distinction presupposed a new understanding of human existence – one that we are still struggling to understand even today. The ancients knew that we are 'natural' realities, like any animal, vegetable or mineral. At the same time they could see that our mind and will are oriented towards the Infinite in a way that other animals seem not to be. This 'supernatural' dimension reveals our rootedness in the Divine. The Jews and especially the early Christians went further than this. They knew that we are not only created by God, but that we 'face' God, because God has turned his own 'face' (*persona*) towards us. In other words, we are not only rational beings, but *persons.* To say that in Christ a human (created) body and soul were assumed not by a human person but by a divine one was to say that in the unique case of Christ, the face that we turned towards God was also the face God turns to us.

By being the mother of Jesus, Mary is necessarily the mother of a *person who is God*, not merely the mother of a human body assumed by God. At the same time, by giving her this title, the Church was defending the idea that motherhood cannot be adequately understood as a biological relationship alone, but is always 'personal'. A woman is not the mother of a body only, or of a human nature, but of a child; that is, always of a person.

This teaching about Mary had cosmic implications. The human nature of Jesus Christ does not exist in splendid isolation, but he takes flesh from a woman. That means he is joined to the material cosmos through his mother. Immediately he becomes vulnerable: what happens to the cosmos, happens to him, and *vice versa.* As God he has entered into it and bears it upon his shoulders; so that when he dies and is resurrected, and when he enters eternal life still in his (transformed) body, the material cosmos – *and first of all things his mother* – is also resurrected, and so can be assumed into heaven. Through the agency of the Holy Spirit, we are joined to this mystery and participate in it. Thus the dogma of Mary's Assumption, followed by her Coronation as Queen of the Universe (the final mystery of the Rosary, which Tolkien discusses in a footnote to Letter 212), though it marks her out as unique among all creatures, is paradoxically not something that isolates her from the rest of mankind.

The Eastern Church Fathers like to use the word *theosis* to describe this process, meaning 'divinisation' or 'deification', and the Catholic *Catechism*, quoting St Thomas, says essentially the same thing (para 460): 'The only-begotten Son of God, wanting to make us sharers in his divinity, assumed our nature, so that he, made man, might make men gods.' In other words, we are intended to become by grace what God is by nature, through participation in his eternal life of love. This precious message – the very heart of the Gospel – along with all that is intimately connected with it, is what is implied by the Church's teaching about the Virgin Mary.

With this as background, we can begin to understand why the Virgin Mary was at the centre of Tolkien's spiritual life. For Catholics, the Virgin is the closest of all creatures to Christ. She is the fairest fruit and flower of creation, the one on whom all the divine gifts are lavished. Whatever Jesus Christ could do for human beings, he did first for his mother. She receives all graces, she is literally 'full of grace'. But divine grace is given only to be passed on, not to be hoarded. She therefore becomes the conduit for the graces that flow from her Son into the whole world. This is what Catholics mean by calling her the Mediatrix: she is the way the cosmos is joined to God.

To his Jesuit friend, Robert Murray, Tolkien wrote: 'I think I know exactly what you mean by the order of Grace, and of course by your references to Our Lady, upon which all my own small perception of beauty both in majesty and simplicity is founded' (L 142). The woman whom Catholics call 'Our Lady' is the centre of a universe of beauty created by her Son. The natural beauties of landscape and forest, mountains and streams, and the moral beauty of heroism and integrity, friendship and honesty – all of which are celebrated in Tolkien's imaginative world – are gifts of God that come through her, and she is the measure of them, her beauty the concentrated essence of theirs.

For Catholics, the Virgin Mary has all the beauty that Eve lost, and just as Eve was the mother of all the living in the world that is past, she is the mother of the world to come. G. K. Chesterton captures this aspect of Our Lady in his poem *The Black Virgin*.

> Clothed with the sun or standing on the moon,
> Crowned with the stars or single, a morning star,
> Sunlight and moonlight are thy luminous shadows,
> Starlight and twilight thy refractions are,
> Lights and half-lights and all lights turn about thee.
> But though we dazed can neither see nor doubt thee,
> Something remains. Nor can man live without it
> Nor can man find it bearable without thee.

STAR OF THE SEA

There is another way in which Mary is present in *The Lord of the Rings*, and that is through her reflections in certain feminine characters, specifically Galadriel and Elbereth. Galadriel is one of the pivotal Elvish characters: bearer of one of the three Rings untouched by Sauron and thereby the preserver of the land of Lothlórien. Tolkien himself calls her 'unstained' in Letter 353 (a word that Catholics normally only use of the Virgin Mary), adding 'she had committed no evil deeds'. He admitted that Catholic teaching and imagination about Mary lay behind the character as portrayed in the novel (L 320). Yet the workings and re-workings of his manuscript reveal an ambiguity here, or at least an evolution, for in earlier drafts she was supposed to be a leader in the rebellion of the Elves against the Valar, the world's angelic guardians. If she was not entirely of Fëanor's party (see p. 85), she was drawn into league with him by a desire to rule lands of her own in Middle-earth.

From this rebellion or this ambition Tolkien later felt the need to absolve her. In Letter 320 (1971) he speaks of her having 'proudly refused forgiveness' at the end of the First Age, but having been pardoned at the end of the Third because of 'her resistance to the final and overwhelming temptation to take the Ring for herself'. (The temptation, of course, played on her desire to rule.) Yet in the *Unfinished Tales*, we find a chapter containing the 'History of Galadriel and Celeborn', in which Christopher Tolkien records the 'late and partly illegible note' which is 'the last writing of my father's on the subject . . . set down in the last month of his life.' In this revised history, which he intended to incorporate in *The Silmarillion*, Galadriel is not at all involved in the rebellion of the Elves but indeed opposed it, and was caught up in the departure from Aman to Middle-earth through no fault of her own. Thus she was morally as well as physically equipped to be the Elvish leader of resistance to Sauron in Middle-earth. We see here, I think, the pressure of the Marian archetype in Tolkien's imagination on the development of the character of Galadriel.

Not quite 'immaculate' (without sin), then, in the official version, but to the hobbits in *The Lord of the Rings* Galadriel is nevertheless a vision of wisdom, beauty, and grace, of light untarnished. Her parting gift to the dwarf Gimli is highly significant. He asks for a single golden hair from her head, which he intends to enshrine within imperishable crystal. In the Elder Days Fëanor had asked the same, and been refused three times, for her tresses were famed for seeming to contain the light of the Two Trees. (The significance of this will be clearer after Chapter 4.). Now she gives Gimli three hairs, one for each of her ancient refusals, which were bound up with so much grief for the Elves. Galadriel's gift heals the long rift between her people and the Dwarves. It implies that she now repents of any part her pride may have played in the long tragedy.

Galadriel, however, remains despite all of this an earthly figure. In Roman Catholic devotion and dogma, the Virgin Mary, having been assumed into heaven at the end of her earthly life, is venerated as Queen of Heaven and 'Star of the Sea'. We find this more cosmic aspect of the Marian archetype expressed in the person of Galadriel's own heavenly patroness, Elbereth, Queen of the Stars, who plays the role in Tolkien's *legendarium* of transmitting light from the heavenly places. It is to Elbereth that the Elves sing their moving invocation:

> O Elbereth! Gilthoniel!
> We still remember, we who dwell
> In this far land beneath the trees,
> Thy Starlight on the Western seas.

Tolkien would have been familiar from his childhood with one of the most popular Catholic hymns to the Virgin Mary, the tone and mood of which are markedly close to that of Tolkien's to Elbereth (see L 213):

> Hail, Queen of Heaven, the ocean star,
> Guide of the wand'rer here below:
> Thrown on life's surge, we claim thy care –
> Save us from peril and from woe.
> Mother of Christ, star of the sea,
> Pray for the wanderer, pray for me.

Starlight on the sea: for Tolkien a particularly evocative combination, as we have seen. Light shining in darkness, representing the life, grace, and creative action of God, is the heart of Tolkien's writing. Light, to him, is always in some sense feminine (remember that in Middle-earth the sun is a 'she'), and Mary the 'universal mediatrix of grace' is present implicitly throughout creation. What is

[57]

earthly beauty other than a light that shines in things and upon things, welling up from within, like the light in Galadriel's phial? The beauties of creation are not those of heaven, but they guide us to their Source as a star may guide us across the ocean: 'For from the greatness and beauty of created things comes a corresponding perception of their Creator' (Wisdom 13:5).

In *Adventures in Orthodoxy*, Dwight Longenecker tellingly describes his reaction to a Raphael Madonna. 'That Raphael painting was full of grace and truth, and I beheld its glory; and that's what Christians say about the relationship between Jesus and God [see John 1:14]. He is God's work of art. He incarnates beauty and truth.' Implicit here is the notion that beauty is *not* exclusively, as we have been told so often, in the eye of the beholder. It lies beyond ourselves, in a sense 'ahead' of us. It is where, deep down, we all want to get to, though we know we have a long way to go. 'That's why we all feel that beauty takes us outside ourselves and puts us in contact with something greater, more mysterious, and more wonderful than we thought existed before,' Longenecker goes on.

> As I gazed on that luminous Madonna, I made contact not only with something beautiful, but with Beauty. It was also an astoundingly intimate experience of purity and power. For a moment I glimpsed a kind of purity that was both as soft as moonlight and as hard as diamonds. I suddenly realized that purity, like all things beautiful and refined, is an acquired taste. Like the fragile beauty of a Mozart aria, or the calm, exquisite beauty of a Chinese vase, purity can be fully sensed only by those who pursue purity themselves, and this realization made my own sordid and tepid life seem small. While looking at the naked child and the Madonna's mysterious smile, I also realized that purity is a hidden and subtle virtue – a precious thing, available only to those who have been given the eyes to see.[8]

There is an echo in this splendid passage of Sam's description of

Galadriel to Captain Faramir, in which Catholics recognise their image of the little girl from Nazareth, crowned with flowers and stars:

> Beautiful she is, sir! Lovely! Sometimes like a great tree in flower, sometimes like a white daffadowndilly, small and slender like. Hard as di'monds, soft as moonlight. Warm as sunlight, cold as frost in the stars. Proud and far-off as a snow-mountain, and as merry as any lass I ever saw with daisies in her hair in springtime.

LADY DAY

Towards the end of *The Lord of the Rings*, when the Ring has been destroyed and Sauron's work undone, Frodo is lying in bed recovering from the ordeal, talking with Gandalf. In Gondor, the wizard tells him, 'the New Year will always now begin upon the twenty-fifth of March when Sauron fell, and when you were brought out of the fire to the King.'

I believe Tom Shippey was the first to point out in this connection that 25 March is the Christian feast day that celebrates the Annunciation: the day when Christ was conceived in the Virgin's womb. It is celebrated with readings that describe Mary's meeting with the Angel Gabriel and her 'yes' to God. This used to be called Lady Day, and was indeed the first day of the year in many parts of Europe. It is exactly nine months before Christmas, because of the time required for the Virgin to come to term and bear her Son.

John Saward cites the following wonderful passage from Honorius of Autun:

> This day is numbered among the chief festivals, because the beginning of the whole Christian religion is dated from it. On this day the world ruined by sin was restored to life by the Passion of Christ. On this day, too, John the Baptist was beheaded, and on this day James, the brother of John, had his

head chopped off. On this sacred day, as the whole Church today celebrates, the Incarnation of Christ was announced by an angel. We read that on this day, at the very hour when the first man was created in paradise, the Son of God, the New Man, was conceived in the Virgin's womb. She was the Paradise of fruit, the *fons hortarum*, because in her sprang forth the Tree of Life, and from her the fount of wisdom flowed forth and poured out all its delights, in whom are hid all the treasures of wisdom and knowledge (cf. Col. 2:3).[9]

Why then did Tolkien choose 25 March for the destruction of the Ring? Well, think again about what the Ring represents. We have already considered it as the archetypal 'Machine'. Viewed theologically the Ring of Power exemplifies the dark magic of the corrupted will, the assertion of self in disobedience to God. It appears to give freedom, but its true function is to enslave us to the Fallen Angel. It corrodes the human will of the wearer, rendering him increasingly 'thin' and unreal; indeed its gift of invisibility symbolises this ability to destroy all natural human relationships and identity, to become untouchable by light.

The person who places himself within the golden circle of the Ring seeks not to be seen, and thereby to have power over others. In this respect it resembles the Ring of Invisibility in the second book of Plato's *Republic* (where Plato interestingly contrasts the 'unjust man' who uses the Ring to steal from others with a 'just man' who is not corrupted by the power it gives, and who ends up being crucified). Through the magic power of the Ring we escape the limitations of matter to enter the world of spiritual forces, but in the very act of doing so we become horribly visible to the forces of evil.

In fact the Ring is partly a symbol of the sin of pride. It draws us towards the Dark Lord by tempting us to become like him. Its circular shape is an image of the will closed in upon itself. Its empty centre suggests the void into which we thrust ourselves by using the Ring. Once there, unseen by others, we are cut off from human contact, removed from the reach of friendship or companionship, anonymous and isolated. The power that the Ring gives is an illusion. It takes us, ultimately, into a world where we are alone with the Eye (the Eye which can see only reflections of itself). In that world of evil there is no room for two wills: the wearer is either absorbed and destroyed, or he defeats Sauron and becomes another Dark Lord himself.[10]

The Ring is sin itself: tempting and seemingly harmless to begin with; increasingly hard to give up and corrupting in the long run. Its destruction, therefore, is a figure of the great reversal of sin achieved at the Annunciation when Mary welcomed the Word of God into our world. Her *fiat*, 'Let it be to me according to your word', overturns the refusal of God's will that we call original sin. That sin also resulted in a kind of invisibility, as Adam hid from the Lord in the forests of Eden: 'But the Lord God called to the man, and said to him, "Where are you?"'

In the National Gallery in London is a small panel painting known as the Wilton Diptych. Commissioned by Richard II, it is one of the most precious and mysterious works of art in England. It shows the king kneeling, surrounded by saints, offering the nation to the Virgin Mary, or perhaps to the baby Jesus who is in her arms, reaching out to receive it. The king is surrounded by a barren and forbidding landscape; but at the feet of Mary the ground is green with grass and bright with flowers,[11] just as the air around her is thronged with angels.

This is the Mary who is ever-present to Tolkien, at the centre of his imagination, mantled by all natural beauty, the most perfect of God's creatures, the treasury of all earthly and spiritual gifts. What Elbereth, Galadriel, and other characters such as Lúthien and Arwen, surely express is precisely what Tolkien said he had found in Mary: *beauty both in majesty and simplicity*. Majesty, for here we see beauty crowned with all the honours that chivalry can bestow; and as for simplicity, well, what is more simple than starlight?

A SACRAMENTAL UNIVERSE

We have seen how the 'religious element' – and even the Catholic element – is absorbed into the symbolism of the stories. But did Tolkien go too far in eliminating religion? Some readers have found it strange that, apart from a lapse into devil-worship by the later Númenoreans, there is seemingly not even any *pagan* religion present in Middle-earth, which is after all set in pre-Christian times. Occasional invocations of Elbereth and the Númenorean grace or 'Standing Silence' before meals hardly constitute a religion.

To this, too, Tolkien had an answer. The peoples of the West described in his stories, he says, descend from Men who escaped from the pagan religion imposed by the Prime Dark Lord, and under the influence of the Elves came into a world of 'pure monotheism'. In that world only Eru was to be given worship, as he was in the far West by the Valar and the Eldar; but no religion could be built around the Valar, and for Men at this time Eru was too remote to be the focus of some ritual form of worship: he had not yet revealed (as he would reveal later to the Jews) how they could build a covenantal relationship with him (L 156). (More detail is supplied in a footnote to Letter 153.)

Tolkien was very careful in trying to construct his world in a way that would faithfully echo the wisdom of the true Creator, as he understood God to be, yet without anticipating the specific content of the Christian revelation. For that revelation had not yet taken place, and 'the Incarnation of God is an *infinitely* greater thing than anything I would dare to write' (L 181).

Within *The Lord of the Rings* (and even within *The Silmarillion*), Tolkien stuck consistently to this principle. The Marian symbolism we have been looking at is no departure from it. It causes no offence to 'pagan' readers, for whom the references to a Lady of the Stars, and the other images of beauty and grace that we find scattered throughout the story, need refer only to an 'eternal feminine' or a goddess of light. As for the Catholic who knows what the author really intends by these evocations, there should be no difficulty regarding them as examples of mediated divine action in the distant past, for the Catholic lives in a symbolic cosmos, in which everything – every stone, every flower, every neighbour – both exists in its own right and symbolises some aspect of the divine.

As Tolkien wrote in 1955 to W. H. Auden: 'each of us is an allegory, embodying in a particular tale and clothed in the garments of time and place, universal truth and everlasting life' (L 163). In this sense the entire natural world is what we might call 'sacramental' – not a sacrament in the strict theological sense, but nevertheless a symbolic system apt for the communication of spiritual realities. 'God speaks to man through the visible creation,' says the *Catechism of the Catholic Church* (para 1147). 'Light and darkness, wind and fire, water and earth, the tree and its fruit speak of God and symbolize both his greatness and his nearness.'

The great exponent of this natural sacramentality is the French Jesuit Jean-Pierre de Caussade (b. 1675). He writes:

> God's love is present in every creature and in every event, just as Jesus Christ and the Church inform us that the sacred body and blood of God are truly present in the Eucharist. His love wishes to unite itself with us through all that the world contains, all that he had created, ordained and allowed. That is his supreme purpose, and to accomplish it he uses both the best and the worst of his creatures, the most unpleasant and the most delightful of happenings.[12]

In this way, God speaks to us through what happens, moment by moment. Even before the birth of Christ, everything that exists and everything that happens has its root in God, and is a 'word' in the divine language. A sense of divine providence, of things meaning more than we know, of coincidences needing to be understood, is of course one of the strongest and most lasting impressions we receive from *The Lord of the Rings*.

The seven sacraments themselves are of course instituted by

Christ much later in time than the events being narrated, and so cannot be directly implied. The divine self-communication in cosmos and history culminates in the Incarnation of Christ, whereby the created world is assumed and healed from within by God himself. The sacraments are symbolic structures that make this Incarnation accessible to the members of the Church. Nevertheless, even these are hinted at within the story. Tolkien justified this by noting: 'far greater things may colour the mind in dealing with the lesser things of a fairy-story' (L 213). In this case of *lembas*, the Elvish 'waybread' that nourishes the will even more than it does the body, and which is more potent when received after fasting, the 'far greater thing' that has influenced Tolkien's story is the Blessed Sacrament, the Eucharist that makes it possible for Christ himself to enter our lives in the form of food.

Tolkien's personal devotion to the Eucharist was intense. He would try to attend Mass each day. (While in Oxford, this would be either at St Aloysius, then in the hands of the Jesuits but today the Oratorians, or the church of St Gregory and St Augustine further up the Woodstock Road.) He writes to his son Michael: 'The only cure for sagging or fainting faith is Communion . . . Frequency is of the highest effect. Seven times a week is more nourishing than seven times at intervals' (L 250). Earlier he had written this moving testament:

> Out of the darkness of my life, so much frustrated, I put before you the one great thing to love on earth: the Blessed Sacrament . . . There you will find romance, glory, honour, fidelity, and the true way of all your loves on earth, and more than that: Death: by the divine paradox, that which ends life, and demands the surrender of all, and yet by the taste (or foretaste) of which alone can what you seek in your earthly relationship (love, faithfulness, joy) be maintained, or take on that complexion of reality, of eternal endurance, which every man's heart desires.

MARRIAGE

It is significant that this passage on the importance of the Eucharist comes at the end of a long letter (L 43) full of advice concerning another key sacrament in Tolkien's life: marriage. There he warns his son against the over-idealisation of these things, and even against the aspiration to find one's 'soul-mate' which has led so many men and women, married and unmarried, into grief. He admits that his own case is exceptional, but hints that even so he is not unacquainted with the frustration and unhappiness that can occur within the best of marriages.[13] Most marriages, even the happiest, can be called 'mistakes' in the sense that (theoretically at least) a more suitable partner might have been found. At one time or another it is likely that tensions will arise. What the married person has to realise is that his 'soul-mate' is not some theoretical alternative partner, or even some real person who is met tragically 'too late', but quite simply the person he is *actually married to*.

The importance Tolkien attached to marriage as a state, and as a spiritual path in life, is evident also in another long letter he drafted to C. S. Lewis, responding to Lewis's suggestion that there should be two sorts of marriage: on the one hand binding Christian wedlock, and on the other a civil marriage that could be dissolved if necessary. He argues that the Christian teaching on marriage (that it should be 'monogamous, permanent, rigidly faithful') cannot be compared to the Muslim teaching on the non-consumption of alcohol, which Lewis had chosen as an example of a religious rule that ought not to be imposed on everybody. Christian marriage and chastity is not a specialised custom or discipline for the few; indeed, if it were not a natural and healthy way for all human beings to live it would be 'an intolerable injustice' to impose it even on Christians (L 49).

In the 1920s another of the Inklings, though an Anglican, had written a defence of indissolubility in *Outlines of Romantic Theology*. Charles Williams there described marriage as not merely a social contract but a 'means of the work of redemption'. Divorce 'is an attempt to nullify a sacrament actually in operation'. 'It is not that it ought not to happen; for Christians it cannot happen, whatever formula is pronounced or ceremonial enacted. When the work is once begun, for better or worse it cannot be stopped.' The 'work' is that of mutual sanctification, which can only be achieved by some form of 'utter surrender' – marriage being one such form.

Marriage occupies an interesting position in the 'sacramental economy' of Christianity, being a sacrament that Christ did *not* institute but simply restored. In the Catholic view, it was created in Paradise, since Adam and Eve were literally made as 'one flesh' in the beginning. Divorce was later permitted by Moses as a concession to the weakness of human nature, but abolished by Jesus (Mark 10:2–12), who came to perfect the law and to supply the grace needed to fulfil it as God had intended. The Catholic Church permits both separation and annulment, but the latter only on the grounds that no true marriage had in fact taken place. That could only happen if one or other partner had not meant or been able to mean the words of the marriage vow, which are carefully chosen to express the *total consent to union of life* that enables God to join together the couple into a new sacramental entity.

Tolkien mentioned in his letter to Lewis that at one time he had '*dissented* in feeling' (though not expressly) from the teaching, and only later come around to appreciating the rightness and the wisdom of it – along with the danger to society in permitting or encouraging any other standard of behaviour. By 1943 the rightness of the teaching was self-evident to him – so much so that it applied even to Elves. During the 1950s he composed a text called 'Laws and Customs Among the Eldar' (to be found in *Morgoth's Ring*) which included details of the marriage customs in Valimar. There we read among other things that 'Marriage is for life, and cannot, therefore, be ended, save by the interruption of death without return.' The Elves, of course, may be killed, but unlike human beings this constitutes for them merely an interruption of earthly life, to which they may return. In that case the re-incarnate is the same person, and the marriage union remains in existence. (The delicate and complex case of second marriages is explored in considerable detail for those who want to take this further.)

Marriage and the Eucharist do not merely happen both to be at the heart of Tolkien's spiritual and moral life: they are intrinsically related, as Charles Williams explains very beautifully in *Romantic Theology*. The union of divine and human natures in Christ at the moment of his conception is itself appropriately called a kind of 'marriage' – being a union that does not dissolve but rather depends upon the distinction of the two elements. Furthermore the passion of Christ on the cross is a 'marriage' of Christ with his spouse the Church (see Eph. 5:32). It signifies the total self-giving of Christ, culminating in the gift of the Holy Spirit of love, which he breathes out with his dying cry in the darkness of Calvary. From this sacrifice of God and Man on the cross, present in the Eucharist, the Holy Spirit is poured out into the world, making the many one.

THE HEART OF A CHiLD

In 1969 Camilla Unwin, daughter of the publisher, wrote to Tolkien in connection with a school project to ask him about the purpose of life. In answer, he took her first through the argument for God's existence (L 310). Of all the approaches people have adopted to this question, the one that appeals to him most is perhaps predictable, given his interest in creativity: it is the 'argument from design'. The world is full of patterns, seeming to proceed from an endlessly creative fountain of invention. But is there truly a mind behind all this? If there is not, then the world is not there for a purpose at all. But if there is, then our knowledge of that mind can be increased by contemplation of it. Perhaps the purpose of our lives is 'to increase according to our capacity our knowledge of God by all the means we have, and to be moved by it to praise and thanks.'

And so we arrive at the heart of Tolkien's spirituality, which he sums up in the *Gloria in Excelsis*: 'We praise you, we call you holy, we worship you, we proclaim your glory, we thank you for the greatness of your splendour.' He continues:

> And in moments of exaltation we may call on all created things to join in our chorus, speaking on their behalf, as is done in Psalm 148, and in The Song of the Three Children in Daniel II. PRAISE THE LORD. . . all mountains and hills, all orchards and forests, all things that creep and birds on the wing.

This touching letter to a child seems to me to say a great deal about the author. His spirituality was one of gratitude and praise – inevitably also a spirituality of childhood, for only the childlike person can truly praise and glory in the wonders of creation that have become so stale to the elderly. In his essay 'On Fairy-Stories' Tolkien cites with approval Andrew Lang's comment: 'He who would enter into the Kingdom of Faerie should have the heart of a little child.' The Virgin Mary who was so central to Tolkien's spiritual life shows us how to have the heart of a child. She was, as Georges Bernanos writes, 'younger than sin'. It is innocence and gentleness, purity and trust, which make us young. The mind withered by cynicism and regret cannot appreciate nature as it comes fresh each day, each moment, from the hand of God.

In the words of G. K. Chesterton's *Orthodoxy*,

> It may not be automatic necessity that makes all daisies alike; it may be that God makes every daisy separately, but has never got tired of making them. It may be that He has the eternal appetite of infancy; for we have sinned and grown old, and our Father is younger than we ('The Ethics of Elfland').

The pure in heart will see God, Christ tells us in the Sermon on the Mount, and the pure are the young. Tolkien remained 'young' enough to write stories for his children and tell them with relish, young enough to chase tourists out of his garden on occasion dressed as an Anglo-Saxon warrior, and young enough to see and love the stars and the leaves in his garden as things which God does not tire of making.

I do not know how closely Tolkien had studied the life of St Philip Neri, the founder of the Oratory to which his guardian Fr Francis Morgan belonged, but the spirituality we can discern in his own life and writings was very close to that of the saint of joy to whom God gave a 'heart of fire' in 1544. Like St Francis more than three hundred years earlier, St Philip was a playful, childlike, musical saint.[14] Undoubtedly we can place Tolkien, through Fr Morgan, in this very clear line of spiritual paternity. Cardinal Newman, too, belonged to it, being the founder of the English Oratory. The way of life of the Oratorians, who were priests living together in community yet not bound by a religious Rule – in some ways a 'collegiate' existence not unlike that of Oxford and Cambridge, though founded on personal friendship – particularly appealed to Newman. As a married layman, Tolkien's life took a different path, but as an Oxford don, a devout Catholic, and a lover of poetry and music, there are more than a few Oratorian resonances in his life.

Another Catholic saint whose spirituality resembles that of Tolkien is the most popular modern 'saint of holy childhood', the Carmelite nun Thérèse of Lisieux. Both Tolkien and Thérèse believed that sanctity can be attained not necessarily, or not only, by the great deeds of mortification and renown with which saints are normally associated, but by the following in fidelity of a 'little way' through daily life, a way set beneath our feet by God. This is again quite similar to the spirituality of Caussade. 'The road goes ever on and on. . .', in the words of Bilbo's walking song, and for Tolkien it is the walking of the road in hope that matters, relying entirely on God's help rather than one's own strength. 'At any minute it is what we are and are doing, not what we plan to be and do that counts' (L 40).

This is Frodo's unassuming kind of heroism, as he volunteers to take the Ring 'though I do not know the way', as he picks his way through the Dead Marshes, and through Shelob's tunnel in total darkness. At times he needs literally to be carried by Sam, as Thérèse said she needed to be carried by God, a small child lifted by her mother or father, up steps that she cannot manage on her own. The Carmelite spirituality of the 'dark night' seems particularly appropriate for Frodo in Mordor, and that blind despair in which he staggers towards Mount Doom, no longer able to visualise or remember light, or fresh water, or any natural beauty.[15]

Frodo is no saint, in the strict sense. Nor are many whose mission takes them through the land of shadow. For them there may be no savour of victory, and even success may feel like a living death. They have been 'too badly hurt'. Yet even unlooked for, in the weariness beyond all conscious hope, the sun may rise. For Frodo, watching from a ship that sails above the bent world, 'the grey rain-curtain turned all to silver glass and was rolled back, and he beheld white shores and beyond them a far green country under a swift sunrise.'

4

LET THESE THinGS BE

Tolkien's 'Middle-earth' is firmly rooted in the 'Midlands' of England. The elements, animals and plants of nature are vividly and lovingly portrayed. His letters, as well as his stories, reveal a man profoundly sensitive to the beauties of the natural world. Here is an example, describing a frosty garden in Oxford after Christmas:

> The rime was yesterday even thicker and more fantastic. When a gleam of sun (about 11) got through it was breathtakingly beautiful: trees like motionless fountains of white branching spray against a golden light and, high overhead, a pale translucent blue. (L 94).

Patrick Curry, in his book *Defending Middle-Earth*, links Tolkien's spirituality to his love of nature. Certainly Tolkien's book was taken up during the 1960s and 70s by the hippies and the Greens opposed to what they called the 'military-industrial complex', and this contributed to its dismissal by the literary establishment as a 'cult book'.

At the same time, Tolkien portrays nature as animated and enchanted in a way that seems at odds with the view normally associated with Christianity. Indeed Curry, who is not a Christian, praises him for this neo-pagan quality. While the descriptions of forests and plains, mountains and storms, changes of light and season, are described so realistically that readers feel they have actually visited

[71]

the landscapes of Middle-earth in the flesh, there is also a sense that more is going on here than meets the eye. The fox who, 'wandering through the wood on business of his own,' stopped and sniffed at the hobbits sleeping under a tree in the open air, remarking to himself, 'There's something mighty queer behind this' (in the chapter 'Three is Company') may have wandered in from another kind of story, but nevertheless it is clear that in Middle-earth birds can be both messengers (of Radagast, for example) and spies (of Saruman), while the very trees – at least in Fangorn and the Old Forest – can move and talk, and the air and water are full of spiritual presences.

It is not entirely fair to accuse the Christian Church, as many still do, of having felled the 'sacred groves' of Europe. Nor can Christianity be blamed for the ecological crisis, for the instruction in Genesis to 'fill the earth and subdue it' need imply nothing more than the exercise of a prudent and priestly stewardship over nature. In many cases the new churches deliberately preserved earlier sacred sites, as Pope Gregory explicitly advised St Augustine to do in England. The idea was that the ancient spirits previously appeased (in some cases) by human or animal sacrifice must now 'bend the knee' to Christ, and their energies must be channelled into the worship of One who came to save nature, not destroy her. The systematic assault on nature had to await a modern era and a new justification.

G. K. Chesterton's biography of St Francis of Assisi explains how the coming of Christianity meant that nature was no longer to be worshipped, but could now be loved in a new way, at least by those who most profoundly understood the true message of the Gospel. 'Man has stripped from his soul the last rag of nature worship, and can return to nature.' It may have been necessary to topple some idols and to cleanse some temples, but by the time of St Francis the 'flowers and stars have recovered their first innocence. Fire and water are felt to be worthy to be the brother and sister of a saint.'[16] It is this Franciscan spirit that permeates Tolkien's writings – and we recall that St Francis and his disciples did on occasion speak to the animals as though they could understand, as did many of the Celtic saints. (Gandalf's fellow-wizard Radagast the Brown, the friend of birds and animals, seems to be a very clear image of St Francis.)

In order to understand the natural world as Tolkien portrayed it in *The Lord of the Rings*, we need to go deeper and read *The Silmarillion*. Tolkien himself felt he had 'been forced to publish upside-down and backwards', and that it would be important for his readers eventually to have things in the right order (L 191). *The Silmarillion* should come first. A bit like an Elvish Old Testament, it is a collection of documents of varying provenance and style, held together roughly in historical sequence. Yet it has a beauty and a splendour of its own that seems to emerge best when read aloud, either to oneself or to others. It was, after all, conceived as the product of a tradition in which the stories would have been sung as poetry. The deluge of Elvish names which immediately engulf the reader form an essential part of the book's charm, for, as we have seen, the root of Tolkien's poetic vision is the language he devised and the thrill of the music that he sensed in words. We are just lucky that we do not have to read the whole work in Elvish, which is what the author would have preferred!

The names, therefore, are very far from being arbitrary labels devised to enable the reader to differentiate the different characters. They have a power of their own when spoken. To most of us, names are opaque; but if we were to read them with Tolkien's sensibility, each would open up for us an interior landscape, evoking the magic of first participation, wherein all things were more transparent to the Word by which they were created.

THE MUSIC OF MEANING

In order to establish the ultimate framework of his *legendarium*, Tolkien composed a creation myth. This is of more than incidental interest: not only does it contain some tremendous writing, but it is the key to understanding the mythology as a whole.

In making this account of the Beginning of Days, Tolkien drew upon many legends that were known to him, and upon the Jewish and Christian traditions that he believed to be true. He was trying to write an account that would be complementary to, while not contradicting, the Genesis story. Any differences from the biblical account were supposed to be due to the fact that it was written not from the human point of view, but from that of the Noldorian Elves through whom it had been transmitted to Bilbo and Sam at Rivendell.

For Tolkien, as a Catholic, God is the Creator of the world *ex nihilo* ('out of nothing'). The world has not always existed. It was not made out of some pre-existing substance. It is not made out of the body of God, in some way divided or parcelled out among creatures. It is not made by two gods. All of these alternatives have been firmly rejected by the Christian tradition. The orthodox teaching is clear: the world – indeed *any conceivable world* – can only have been made by the One God from nothing. In both the Bible and *The Silmarillion*, the physical world is created by the word of God. In the Elvish account, however, there are three preceding stages, the first of which involves the creation of the Ainur or 'Holy Ones'. The second stage is the proposing of themes and the singing of a great music by Eru and the Ainur together.

I suppose the central importance Tolkien gives to music (as does C. S. Lewis, if you recall Aslan 'singing' Narnia into existence in *The Magician's Nephew*) may have been suggested to him by some famous lines in the Book of Job. 'Where were you . . . when the morning stars sang together, and all the sons of God shouted for joy' (Job 38:7), God asks Job in the Authorised Version – or 'when the morning stars praised me together, and all the sons of God made a joyful melody' in the Douay-Rheims translation familiar to Catholics of Tolkien's generation. At any rate, as Verlyn Flieger remarks in *Splintered Light*, 'For Tolkien, as for medieval man, light and music are conjoined elements manifest in the music of the spheres, the singing of the stars.'[17]

Tolkien's 'Ainulindalë', the Elves' account of the creation of the world, begins as follows:

> There was Eru, the One, who in Arda [the Earth] is called Ilúvatar; and he made first the Ainur, the Holy Ones, that were the offspring of his thought, and they were with him before aught else was made. And he spoke to them, propounding to them themes of music; and they sang before him, and he was glad.

Melkor, the highest and most gifted of the Ainur (equivalent to Lucifer in Christian terminology) begins to rebel, by interweaving 'matters of his own imagining that were not in accord with the theme of Ilúvatar; for he sought therein to increase the power and glory of the part assigned to himself.' The discord spreads through the music until it resembles a raging storm. In response, Ilúvatar intervenes three times. The first time he smiles as he introduces a second theme into the music, but Melkor again prevails, and frowning he introduces a third theme 'at first soft and sweet, a mere rippling of gentle sounds in delicate melodies; but it could not be quenched, and it took to itself power and profundity.' This is the theme of Elves and Men, the 'Children of Ilúvatar'. The third and final time that Ilúvatar intervenes, as Melkor's discord drowns out both new themes, is in order to end the music.

Eru then translates the music into the form of a great vision, displayed in the void. Now the Ainur are able to see the meaning of the music they have been making. They see how it can be embodied in a world of living creatures, interwoven destinies, composed of elements and forces unfolding in time. The Ainur are drawn towards this newly-created world by a love of beauty.

> [They] looked upon this habitation set within the vast spaces of the World, which the Elves call Arda, the Earth; and their hearts rejoiced in light, and their eyes beholding many colours were filled with gladness; but because of the roaring

of the sea they felt a great unquiet. And they observed the winds and the air, and the matters of which Arda was made, of iron and stone and silver and gold and many substances; but of all these water they most greatly praised. And it is said by the Eldar that in water there lives yet the echo of the Music of the Ainur more than in any substance else that is in this Earth; and many of the Children of Ilúvatar hearken still unsated to the voices of the Sea, and yet know not for what they listen.

Knowing the desire in the hearts of the Ainur for this beauty to become 'real' in the same way that they are themselves, Eru sends forth the secret fire, and kindles the world into actuality with the divine command:

> *'Eä!* Let these things Be! And I will send forth into the Void the Flame Imperishable, and it shall be at the heart of the World, and the World shall Be; and those of you that will may go down into it.'
>
> And suddenly the Ainur saw afar off a light, as it were a cloud with a living heart of flame.

Verlyn Flieger, ever conscious of the importance of words for Tolkien, writes that: '*The Silmarillion* is testimony to his desire to "explore the implications of one word", for the whole vast sweep of his mythology is in truth just that – the exploration of the implications and ramifications of the one word *Eä.* '[18]

But how does this account square with the one we find in the Book of Genesis? For Tolkien, God's act of creation can be broken down into four stages:

1. thought (the Ainur),
2. music (which also involved the angelic fall),
3. light in the void (when the music is translated into vision), and finally
4. being, or material existence.

On the other hand, the Genesis account starts as follows:

> In the beginning God created the heaven and the earth. And
> the earth was without form, and void; and darkness was upon
> the face of the deep. And the spirit of God moved upon the
> face of the waters. And God said, 'Let there be light': and
> there was light. And God saw the light, that it was good: and
> God divided the light from the darkness (Gen. 1:1–4, AV).

The main point of Genesis seems to be identical with that of the
Elvish account: that there is One God, who is the sole and supreme
Creator of all things seen and unseen. Notice that even before God's
word pronounced over the face of the deep causes light to spring into
existence, there is mention of three other 'things' in Genesis, if we
can call them that, which seem already to have been made by God:

1. heaven (or 'heaven-and-earth'),
2. earth (a formless void), and
3. the 'waters' over which the Spirit of God is moving.

If there is a direct correspondence to each of these in Tolkien's
account it is probably to:

1. the Ainur,
2. the formless void that surrounds them, and
3. the song.

Of these the song is perhaps the most intriguing. If the deep mentioned in Genesis is the primordial substance of creation, the sea of
potentiality, then the music of the Ainur could be said to be the pattern of vibration created on the surface of the deep by the 'spirit' of
God. And so we 'hearken still unsated to the voices of the Sea', and
know not for what we listen.

Another biblical account of creation is found in the Prologue to
the Gospel of John:

> In the beginning was the Word, and the Word was with God,

and the Word was God. The same was in the beginning with God. All things were made by him; and without him was not any thing made that was made. In him was life; and the life was the light of men. And the light shineth in darkness; and the darkness comprehended it not (John 1:1–4, AV).

Here John deepens the earlier account of creation. Genesis speaks of 'the spirit of God', but it is unclear whether this is a separate divine person from the 'God' referred to in the first sentence. John, on the other hand, speaks of the 'Word' (Greek: *Logos*) who is 'with' God yet also 'is' God, and this is intended as a reference to the divine nature of Christ, the Son of God. *Logos* also means 'harmony', 'order' and 'meaning'.

For Christian theology, based on the events recorded in the gospels and reflection upon these by the early Christians, God is one divine 'substance' yet three divine persons. Father, Son and Spirit are each the same God, yet distinct from each other in a way that does not divide them into three separate things. Tolkien's account cannot be explicitly Trinitarian, for it is supposed to pre-date the Christian and even the Judaic revelation. What it does instead is explore 'behind' God's act of creating the *World that Is*, and find there a spiritual creation preceding the physical. The corporeal world embodies a vision, the vision embodies a music, and the music is the harmony of the Ainur who are the offspring of divine thought.

THE GODS OF MIDDLE-EARTH

The Elvish account of creation is close to some versions of Platonic cosmology, but it should be noted that each succeeding stage, though it manifests the one before it, is no mere 'echo' or diminished reflection of the one before – as it might be in a scheme that described the world as some kind of automatic emanation from God, radiating out into the void. At each stage God *adds* something that was not there before. The music is something 'proposed' to the

Ainur, in which they have the freedom to express their own natures and even to try to rebel. The vision leaves the Ainur 'amazed'. The world, again, is more than the vision: 'and they knew that this was no vision only, but that Ilúvatar had made a new thing: Eä, the World that Is.' It is real, now, in the same sense that they are.

In an unfinished letter (212 in the published collection), Tolkien describes this as differing somewhat from most Christian accounts of the Creation, in that the angelic fall takes place before the creation of the material world, and consequently a tendency to evil is able to enter into the world 'already when the *Let it Be* was spoken' by Ilúvatar. However, the fall of Lucifer to become the 'Satan' normally identified with the serpent in the Garden is only hinted at, never described in the Bible. The Christian (and Jewish) tradition has embellished the account of Genesis, using other hints scattered throughout Scripture (including the reference of Jesus to having seen Satan fall 'like lightning from heaven'), but it never definitively established whether the angelic fall took place before or after the creation of matter. Lewis and Tolkien had therefore speculated that a prior, angelic fall would help to explain the great sufferings we observe in nature, which are hard to attribute entirely to the fall of man.

Tolkien, of course, has no doubt that evil is the result of free decisions by a created nature that was good at the outset. Matter itself, and the natural world, are both originally good, albeit corrupted. Furthermore, whilst the evil that is done by Melkor may destroy the original design of the Creator and mar the creation at every level, the eventual victory of Ilúvatar is certain, for even the work of the Fallen One will somehow prove 'a part of the whole and tributary to its glory'. Ilúvatar tells them that 'no theme may be played that hath not its uttermost source in me, nor can any alter the music in my despite. For he that attempteth this shall prove but mine instrument in the devising of things more wonderful, which he himself hath not imagined.'

The Ainur who descend to play the parts they have chosen within the history of Earth, contending from the outset against the chaos introduced by the dark Angel, are called Valar (Powers). They are accompanied by numerous attendant spirits called Maiar, some of whom later have key roles in Middle-earth (Sauron, Gandalf, Saruman).

The sky god Manwë is the chief of the Valar and closest to Ilúvatar. Paired with him is Varda or Elbereth, the goddess of light and Lady of the Stars. Ulmo is the Lord of Waters, dwelling alone in the oceans and rivers. Aulë is the Lord of material substance and the 'smith' of the gods; he is paired with Yavanna, the Giver of Fruits and goddess of growing things, known to the Elves as Queen of the Earth. The others include the warrior god Tulkas, the hunter Oromë, and Mandos who is the keeper of the Houses of the Dead.

Resemblances to the Roman and Greek pantheon, and the Norse gods of Asgard, are obvious: Zeus, Poseidon, Aries, Hades, and several others are present and accounted for. But the differences are striking too. The old gods' rough edges have gone, the lustful squabbling of the Olympians is notable for its absence, and the presence of a supreme deity beyond even Manwë is explicitly affirmed. Manwë himself (unlike Zeus) 'has no thought for his own honour, and is not jealous of his power, but rules all to peace'. In other words, Tolkien has integrated the ancient pagan conception of deity with a Christian understanding of the world. His proposal is that the supposedly more ancient Elvish 'histories' contain more accurate information about the gods than many of the mythological guesses made by man.

Tolkien's pantheon embodies, in concentrated form, his poetic insight into the natural cosmos. As such it repays not only close attention, but repeated meditation. In some sense he may have actually believed in these Powers, or at least something like them. Certainly he had a basis for doing so in Christian teaching about the Nine Choirs of Angels (Seraphim, Cherubim, Thrones, Dominations, Virtues, Powers, Principalities, Archangels and Angels). The Roman Catholic tradition is firm on the existence of a hierarchy of created spirits or Intelligences that are involved (always under God's overall direction or orchestration) in the building and administration of creation. The modern *Catechism of the Catholic Church* reaffirms this tradition. In fact the Church teaches that one of the lesser spirits is assigned to every human being as a guardian and guide through life, and as a companion after death: Catholics are encouraged to pray to their guardian angel every day, and Tolkien most probably did so.

A rare glimpse of this essentially private type of experience is afforded by a letter (L 89) in which he describes a vision he received whilst praying before the Blessed Sacrament in a traditional devotion called the 'Forty Hours'. He perceived a speck or mote suspended in the Light of God. The mote was himself, 'or any other human person that I might think of with love', and the experience was accompanied by a great sense of joy. The mote was glittering white in the ray connecting it to the source of Light, and that ray was nothing less than the guardian angel of the mote, the expression of God's living attention directed towards that particular person. In another letter (54) he writes of the guardian angel as supporting us, as it were 'from behind', giving us the strength to face God freely for ourselves, like a spiritual umbilical cord or life-line.

This sensitive awareness of the angels is reminiscent of John Henry Newman, whose sermon on 'The Powers of Nature' is a beautiful evocation of the role of the Ainur in the world we see around us, operating behind the phenomena observed by science.

> I affirm, that as our souls move our bodies, be our bodies what they may [according to science], so there are Spiritual Intelligences which move those wonderful and vast portions of the natural world which seem to be inanimate . . . Every breath of air and ray of light and heat, every beautiful prospect, is, as it were, the skirts of their garments, the waving of the robes of those whose faces see God in heaven.[19]

For Tolkien, and other members of his circle,[20] the angels are like

Plato's Forms (Justice, Man, Rose and so on), but they are *alive*; they have *free will*. As living creatures distinct from the divine Essence, they pre-exist the world of time – which simply means that the world is made to exist through an act of God that includes them as secondary causes in its shaping and composition. The freedom of the angels means that they can turn against God. The very structure of the world becomes a drama of freedom and choice.

The concept of living ideas can perhaps be traced to the Pythagoreans, for whom Numbers were living gods. The music of the Ainur is probably equivalent to the 'music of the spheres' in this long tradition. But there is a great profundity in the novel idea introduced by Tolkien that the angels themselves, in his account, *do not hear the end of the music*, but must await its fulfilment along with the whole creation. The beauty of what God is to accomplish in world history surpasses the harmony of the spheres itself.

AGES OF LIGHT AND DARKNESS

The Powers who choose to enter into Arda as 'Valar' initially shape it according to their own conceptions of beauty, taming its tumults and making of it a 'garden for their delight'. With the arrival of Melkor, however, they are forced to strive for mastery, and the world is torn and shaken, losing its early symmetry. Aware from the music that the Children of Ilúvatar (Elves and Men) are destined to arise in the course of time, the Valar need to make it safe for these more fragile creatures. Unwilling to risk excessive damage to the fabric of Arda, therefore, they allow themselves to be driven into the West, where they build up the land of Aman, the city of Valinor and the great mountain of Taniquetil crowned with stars.

Much of the later drama is shaped by this 'retreat' of the gods from the centre of the world into the West. There is some suggestion in the posthumously published writings that Tolkien believed this to be a 'mistake' of the gods, showing a lack of faith in Ilúvatar. If they had known all that would befall as a result of abandoning Middle-earth to Melkor at a crucial time in its history they would have held their ground. Of course, as we know, even the mistakes and mis-judgments of the gods are worked by Ilúvatar into his greater design. The gradual removal of the numinous world of the gods from Middle-earth, until it is finally taken away from the realm of the Visible altogether, seems by hindsight an inevitable process. We stand at a later point in the music, and its design has begun to be revealed to us. However, the gods were not compelled to adopt the course they did. Like us, but in their own higher sphere of action, they had the freedom to do to do otherwise.

We are now out of the Ages of Creation and into a later but still 'pre-historic' or mythical period, each successive age of which is named after its main source of light. For as Verlyn Flieger has revealed so clearly, the concrete metaphor of light and its history gives an underlying structure to Tolkien's mythos. The light of Arda comes first from two great Lamps, raised by the gods above the north and the south of the world. After these are cast down by Melkor, only Aman is illuminated, this time by the gently modulated radiance of two trees grown by the song of Yavanna – first a silver tree called Telperion and then a golden called Laurelin, their liquid light being hoarded in 'great vats like shining lakes'.

While the Trees still shine in Aman, the Age of the Stars begins in Middle-earth. Varda/Elbereth now sets new and brighter stars and constellations in the sky, made from the silver dews of Telperion, as light for the Children of Ilúvatar when they awake. In his impatience to see the Children, Aulë makes intelligent creatures of his own: the Seven Fathers of the Dwarves. He is rebuked by Ilúvatar, who never-theless grants the Dwarves the independent life and free will that is his to give. (For Tolkien the creation of a soul is always a direct intervention of God, akin to the first making of the world itself.)[21] When the Elves at last arise silently on the shores of Cuiviénen, hearing the sound of running water, the stars are the first things they see: 'Therefore they have ever loved the starlight, and have revered Varda Elentári [Star-kindler] above all the Valar', and they associated this for ever with the sound of water. (Elves can of course see perfectly well by starlight.)

The Elves are known as 'those that speak with voices' (Quendi). As Treebeard points out, it is they who begin to name things and to devise language. The language they invent is itself a response to light – fitting enough in a world that begins with the unity of music, light and *Logos* (Word). Against the background of Owen Barfield's theory of the evolution of consciousness, Verlyn Flieger writes: 'Consciousness, expressed in speech, is relationship to light' (p. 70). We would also do well to recall the fact that the phenomenon of light remains mysterious even today; that is, even to modern science. The optics of Isaac Newton was based on the splitting of white light into many colours (a departure, as Gandalf emphasises to Saruman, from the path of wisdom). But when Einstein built his theory of relativity around the fact that the speed of light remained constant no matter what the velocity of the observer, the old Cartesian/Newtonian mechanistic understanding of light had effectively been transcended. In 1951 Einstein wrote that after fifty years of thinking about it, he was no closer to understanding what light actually is – *and nor was anyone else.*

This 'absolute' quality of light in modern physics recalls aspects of the medieval and ancient view of light as the primal form of corporeity and the expression of the first divine Word. The medieval world was built out of light, and this light was understood as an expression of God's creative act of 'seeing'. The poetic thrill we feel when a modern astronomer tells us that the elements of our bodies are made from stardust, having been forged in the heavenly furnaces millennia ago, is surely a faint echo of that ancient insight. Until the modern period, too, it was commonly assumed in a tradition that derived from the Greeks that the human eye saw by virtue of a spiritual fire or light residing within it, which rayed out to meet and merge with the light of the world. Tolkien writes from within that tradition, as anyone can tell from reading *The Lord of the Rings*, which abounds in descriptions of eyes glowing and shining. This is more than an over-used metaphor: it fits a mythology that is, among other things, an account of the entwined history of light, consciousness and language.

With the arrival of the Elves, we have come also to the creation of the 'Silmarils' which give their name to the saga as a whole. These holy jewels represent an incarnation of the light that comes from heaven, in a form that can be grasped by creatures of the earth. Their maker, Fëanor, a prince of the Noldorian Elves and their greatest craftsman, fills them with liquid light from the Two Trees in Valinor. What is most desirable about the Silmarils is not therefore their crystalline form but the light that lives in them, which is itself not a creation of the artist but a gift from the gods. Fëanor's 'greedy love' for the work of his hands (they represent, after all, the highest point attainable by both art and science) marks the Fall of the Elves, for 'sin' involves attempting to take possession of such gifts, and forgetting to hold them in trust and gratitude. If the drama of time is the use and misuse of freedom, the jewels are at the centre of that drama.

The Fall of the Elves is expressed outwardly in the stealing of the Silmarils by Melkor, now named 'Morgoth', the Enemy. At the same time the Trees are destroyed, sucked dry and poisoned by the spider-creature Ungoliant, personification of Morgoth's envy: the desire of darkness for the light. The radiance of the Trees remains only in the Silmarils, which Fëanor and his sons vow to pursue with vengeance and hatred to the end of the world, withholding them even from the Valar. This terrible oath turns them also against the other Elves, and drives them into exile. Middle-earth is now centre stage. It is there that the drama continues to unfold, and it does so under a new dispensation of light, for the Moon and Sun are fashioned from the last fruit of the dying Trees, and three long Ages of the Sun begin: the first Age revolving around the defeat of Morgoth, the Second the rise and fall of Númenor, and the Third the War of the Ring.

These three cycles each express the fate of light on a new level. We are moving, if you like, from mythical towards historical time, and in consciousness from the primal unity towards a fragmented, externalised universe. Men arise for the first time under the light of the Sun. Their early years are unknown to the Elves and therefore not recorded.[22] In the First Age of the Sun, the Silmarils are regained but then placed beyond reach, while the memory of the ancient light enters the bloodstream of Men through Beren and Eärendil. In the Second Age, the pursuit of the light still lingering in the West becomes confused with earthly glory. After the drowning of Númenor, Middle-earth is cut off from the West and all it represents. In the Third Age, the interior light now hidden in the bloodline of the Dúnedain must emerge through the destruction of the Ring which threatens to engulf it, becoming the spiritual foundation for an Age of Men.

It is worth noting that the conception of time demonstrated here is both cyclic and linear. Each cycle repeats certain themes and patterns, but with important variations, just as might occur in a musical composition. From one point of view we see nothing but declension from an initial state of purity and concentration; from another we see a series of advances in complexity. Both points of view are enfolded within an ordered unity that can only be perceived as beautiful, when it is grasped as a whole, as a *gestalt*.

Owen Barfield believed that the European tradition had broken from the repetitive cycles we find in the world of ancient myth and ritual largely thanks to the Hebrews. While the Greeks had dis-covered form in space, the Hebrews had discovered form in time. Through the Jewish and Christian tradition God had revealed a linear pattern in history. It was no longer simply an earthly copy of some heavenly archetype, it was *going somewhere*. Myth gave way to history. But Barfield added that only modern consciousness had made the mistake of assuming a narrative must be *either* an histori-cal record *or* a symbolical representation, thus eliminating the cyclic element altogether. For Barfield and Tolkien the best narratives were both.

DEATH AND IMMORTALITY

The many stories in *The Silmarillion* from the three Ages of the Sun are largely concerned with another theme, as important as that of the history of light, which emerges particularly strongly in the contrast between Men and Elves. The new theme is *death*, and the various ways of escaping or accepting it (see L 212). Tolkien, of course, had a particularly strong sense of mortality, thanks to the early death of his parents and his experience of the War in which he and C. S. Lewis lost most of their close friends. This personal fascination with the meaning of death helps to endow his mythology with a serious-ness and even urgency that is rare in fantasy writing. He was wrestling with a universal human concern, and consequently his mythology becomes a vehicle to explore the human condition itself.

Tolkien realised that the yearning for the light from which we came, for a lost Golden Age, an age of innocence, is intimately connected with the desire for immortality. The sense of universal entropy, of falling away, of sliding into decay, of losing one's great-ness, of becoming old and grey, is all part of the 'taste' of death. Our desire for immortality is not really for that slow decline to be even slower. It is not, when we get right down to it, a desire to be merely *extended*, to be spread like a small piece of butter over too much bread (to use Bilbo's analogy). The Ring promises an immortality of that kind, but a life of servitude to the Ring is no better than a living death. The real desire for immortality, on the other hand, is healthy; it is a desire to overcome the process of decline itself. It is a desire not to extend but to *transcend* time.

A great many people these days believe in reincarnation. They believe it in the form taught by the Theosophical Society: the soul moves from body to body in order to educate itself and to evolve beyond the human state, eventually liberating itself entirely from matter and becoming one with the universal Spirit or Cosmic Consciousness. The idea of 'liberation from matter' is reminiscent of the ancient heresy of Gnosticism, but it has a particular appeal to

Westerners who since Descartes have been accustomed to thinking of the mind as a ghostly passenger or pilot in the machine of the body, and since the nineteenth century of all life in a continual process of evolution. It also appears to many people as an attractive and merciful alternative to the Christian teaching that we only have one life and one chance to escape the eternal fires of hell.

In its original Asian form, the theory of reincarnation was both more complex and less consoling. Reincarnation as a *human being* was regarded as an extremely rare chance. If that life was squandered by bad living, a second chance was not the immediate result: more likely would be a series of lifetimes in one of the hells or as one of the lower animals. In Buddhist versions of the teaching, it is not so much metaphysical as therapeutic, designed to enlist the imagination in a process of progressive detachment from desire.

In any case, even the popular doctrine of reincarnation is not as consoling as it first appears. A person who believes in reincarnation is often unable to find much comfort after the death of a loved one in the idea that the beloved is once again an infant and has completely forgotten his previous life. Deep down, we all want something rather different: a continuation of personality and of relationships.

Christians who wish to accommodate a belief in reincarnation are obliged to reject the clear teaching of the saints, and assume that the Gospels (in which Christ speaks of an eternal hell as a real possibility) must at some point have been deliberately falsified. Reincarnation is therefore incompatible with Catholic, Orthodox or Evangelical Christianity, which take seriously Christ's promise that his Spirit will remain with the Church until the end of time, guiding it into the truth. Tolkien, as a practising Catholic, must have found Barfield's acceptance of the doctrine one of the more bizarre aspects of his devotion to Rudolf Steiner (a former Theosophist).

Tolkien did not, however, see anything wrong with exploring the idea in the world of his imagination, and made good use of it in constructing the drama of the Elves. The Elves are immortal, in the sense that they do not die of old age or illness, and if murdered can be 'sent back' from the Halls of Mandos to resume their life on earth. Their fate is not to depart from the world, but to remain for as long as it exists, if not in fully embodied form, then in a kind of limbo or waiting state. Only when the world itself ends would they face the great mystery of what lies beyond Time; but for the whole life of the world they are bound within it, and can only be parted from their bodies temporarily.

At first Tolkien assumes the Elves' normal way of return will be by being reborn as a child. However, in later writings this changes. Tolkien was perhaps too conscious of the way our embodiment within a family and a set of relationships helps to make us who we are. Reincarnation would imply too great a change in the *hröa* (body) of the elf to be consistent with real self-identity. Tolkien concluded that this return must be in the form of resurrection rather than reincarnation. The 'resurrection body' would be a kind of thought-form, based on the memory of his first embodied state. It would be able to pass through matter at will, but it could also become tangible if desired.

The temptation of the Elves is always to a kind of melancholy, for the Elves are the great appreciators and stewards of nature, but being blessed with an unfailing memory they are also burdened with a sense of transience and loss. Their music reflects this, because music is an art of transience and change, and their songs express both a love for the patterns of time and an attempt to capture, celebrate and repeatedly invoke them. As time goes by the weight of memory increases, and correspondingly the importance of the present and the future seems to dim. (The Elves 'remain until the end of days, and their love of the Earth and all the world is more single and more poignant therefore, and as the years lengthen ever more sorrowful.') Men, on the other hand, look mostly to the future, and their temptation is not to halt time but to extend it – to conquer it, ultimately, by manufacturing more and more: by postponing death in every way possible.

Ilúvatar has decreed that the destiny of Men lies somewhere else, a mystery both to the Elves and to themselves. 'Therefore he willed that the hearts of Men should seek beyond the world and should find no rest therein.' Christians will recognise here an echo of St Augustine's famous phrase; 'Thou hast made us for Thyself, and our hearts are restless till they rest in Thee.' But one important divergence from the usual Christian description of reality should be noted, namely that death is here no punishment for Original Sin, but a great gift and an inherent part of the nature of Man.

Writing in 1954, Tolkien himself seems unsure whether or not this could be construed as heretical (L 156), but by 1958 he had arrived at an explanation that seemed to satisfy him. In Letter 212 he writes that the account of death in *The Silmarillion* reveals *the Elvish view* of how death should be viewed, even if it was originally inflicted on Men as a punishment. Once accepted, any divine punishment – which is, after all, intended as a blessing, for it corrects a fault – can also be seen as a 'gift'. The Creator is, after all, supremely creative, and when forced by the rebellion of his creatures to alter the design of the world (in this case by imposing the punishment of death as a consequence of human sin), he will bring out of that change a new and perhaps an even greater good.

The fate of Men is to leave the world behind after a brief life, and not to return as the Elves do, but to continue into a mystery that is 'more than memory'. The last king of Númenor rejects this fate, and, seeking an impossible immortality, sets foot on the shore of the Blessed Lands, bringing down catastrophe upon his people. The earth is made round, so that the sea-road to the West never reaches it but returns in a circle to the place where it began. The Elves will now be able to sail the Straight Road from Middle-earth to Valinor only by a special grace of the Valar.

The drowning of Númenor by a gigantic wave in Tolkien's famous recurrent dream was an important source of his inspiration. That image is also one of the purest and most powerful images of death and loss in all of literature. Drowning by an unstoppable wave is the speeded-up version of the Thing that faces all of us, though we contrive to forget it for a while.

Given its centrality in Tolkien's mythology as the link between the world of today and the Elder Days when the world was flat, between mythical time and historical time, the drama of Númenor and its progeny lies at the heart of his work. Shaped like a great five-pointed star, the island known as the 'Land of Gift' represents the mingling of earth and heaven in the midst of the sea – another image of buried and fragmented light. But the tragedy of Númenor points in two directions: forward and back. Forward lies the story of Aragorn and Arwen, familiar from *The Lord of the Rings*. For Aragorn is the heir of Elendil, leader of the survivors from Númenor. He bears on his brow the 'Star of the Dúnedain', which recalls his ancestor Eärendil, the father of the first King of Númenor, Elros, the brother of Elrond. But backward, behind both these stories, lies the tale of Beren and Lúthien, and with this we come even closer to the source of Tolkien's inspiration.

The tale is crucial to an understanding of Tolkien's spirituality, and for that reason among others I suggest that you go and read the relevant sections of *The Silmarillion*, or its longer, earlier and poetic form in *The Lays of Beleriand* (third volume of 'The History of Middle-Earth'). All I can provide here is the barest of outlines, and the texture and detail of the story are much richer than I am able to suggest. Perhaps when the story is one day made into a film, it will receive the attention it deserves.

Set in the First Age, the story tells how love first binds together Man and Elf, and creates a new, and indeed superior, hybrid strain uniting the two races known in the *legendarium* as the Children of Ilúvatar. The term 'Half-Elven' is most familiar to us as the title of Elrond, the wise master of the Last Homely House, whom we meet in *The Hobbit*. When Tolkien first wrote that book, he may only have had the dimmest inkling (pardon the pun) that the lord of Rivendell would emerge in the greater works as the son of Eärendil, and brother to the kings of Númenor.

In brief, then, Beren, a mortal man, falls in love with Lúthien, the daughter of the Elf-King Thingol. To get rid of this unwelcome and unworthy human suitor, Thingol sends him on an impossible quest: to bring him a Silmaril from Morgoth's crown. He succeeds, with Lúthien's help, but loses first his hand, and then his life (defending Thingol). Lúthien follows him to the underworld, and sings to the Lord of Death the most beautiful song in the world, a song that weaves together the griefs of the Two Kindreds. If the world is founded on song, this is its central theme. Moved to tears, Mandos permits Lúthien to reject the fate of the Elves in favour of a human death, in order to be with him for ever. Her decision will open the way for others, including Arwen, to choose the same destiny. The couple return to life in Middle-earth, before their final journey into the unknown. In time they die once more, although 'none marked where at last their bodies lay'.[23]

The second marriage of Elves and Men takes place in the hidden Elvish kingdom of Gondolin. The man Tuor bears a prophetic message from Ulmo about its peril. But its king does not heed the warning, though he permits Tuor to marry his daughter. Gondolin is betrayed from within, the last of the Elvish kingdoms in Middle-earth to fall. Its spectacular destruction by a massive assault of orcs, dragons and balrogs was one of the first parts of the *legendarium* composed by Tolkien, and was eventually published in the second part of the 'Book of Lost Tales'. The remnants of Gondolin, including Tuor's son Eärendil, escape to the coast, where they join the people of Elwing, grand-daughter of Beren and Lúthien, to whom Eärendil is soon wedded. Thanks to the Silmaril which Elwing has inherited, and his own remarkable ancestry, Eärendil is permitted to plead before the Valar on behalf of all the free peoples of Middle-earth. His plea is answered, and the Valar descend upon Middle-earth in a war of wrath that destroys the power of Morgoth.

The Silmaril is set upon the brow of the immortal Eärendil as he sails the darkness of space in a silver ship fashioned for him by the Valar. It is in this form, as a beam of light from the Morning and

Evening Star, captured in a crystal phial, that the same light much later comes to Frodo as a gift from Fëanor's cousin Galadriel. The two remaining Silmarils, at last retrieved from Morgoth's crown, are stolen from the Valar by the surviving sons of Fëanor, only to be buried in the sea and in the fires of the earth at the end of the First Age – separated until the end of Time.

From this overview we see the way Tolkien evoked the tragedy and the mystery of death against the backdrop of the greater mystery of existence itself. The sense of loss, of a world passing away, fills *The Lord of the Rings* and *The Silmarillion* like the sound of the sea and the glimmer of starlight; but for there to be loss, there must first have been possession. The destruction of the Trees, the successive falls of Menegroth, Nargothrond, Gondolin and Númenor, leading to the removal of Valinor, add layer upon layer to the mood of nostalgia evoked by Galadriel in the song she sings to Frodo, a song of the Noldor in exile:

> '. . . Now lost, lost to those from the East is Valimar!
> Farewell! Maybe thou shalt find Valimar.
> Maybe even thou shalt find it. Farewell!'

It is a nostalgia for something real. Through myth, through poetry, Tolkien has evoked a feeling beyond words that comes from the deepest levels of our nature, a yearning which God has implanted within us. That feeling is a sign that we are called back to a light, and a music, and a Word that contain and transcend the pattern and the meaning of the world. The Elves can hope for nothing higher than memory: a frozen image of perfect beauty in the Far West. And if Tolkien had not been a Christian, perhaps this would have been something like his final word. But Men are not Elves, and the hope of Men does truly reach further.

'In sorrow we must go, but not in despair,' Aragorn tells Arwen. 'Behold! we are not bound for ever to the circles of the world, and beyond them is more than memory.'

The death of Man involves a definitive departure from this world into an unknown future. When it becomes a choice – for Lúthien, for Arwen – it is an act of faith in the Maker of all things, and in the love he has placed within the human heart. In the end only the Creator can triumph over Morgoth, whose will precipitates the tragedy of the fall. This he will do, *The Silmarillion* hints, not by forcing the free will of his creatures, but by weaving their own failures and sins into a yet greater design of his own.

5

BEHIND THE STARS

> The Light of Valinor (derived from light before any fall) is
> the light of art undivorced from reason, that sees things both
> scientifically (or philosophically) and imaginatively (or sub-
> creatively) and 'says that they are good' – as beautiful.
>
> *J. R. R. Tolkien to Milton Waldeman (L 131 fn)*

What Tolkien sensed behind the folklore and languages of the North
and in fragments of Anglo-Saxon poetry can be given a name: it is
'Elvishness'. Like 'Orcishness' this is an element in human nature,
these two contrasting strands representing the spiritual possibilities
of humanity in our own time.

> The Elves represent, as it were, the artistic, aesthetic, and
> purely scientific aspects of the Humane nature raised to a
> higher level than is actually seen in Men. (L 181).

At one level, then, the Elves represent an ideal way of relating to
the natural world. They are artists, but also scientists and nature-
mystics: they have a love, intense and intimate, for the trees and
flowers, the hills and rivers, the winds and sounds of this earth,
which they cherish, celebrate and try to preserve with their magic.

Tolkien traced Elvishness back to the point where Elves and Men
first come together: 'The story of Beren and Lúthien,' he writes
(L 156 fn), 'is the way by which "Elvishness" becomes wound in as
a thread in human history.' In this final chapter I want to examine

Elvishness – what it is, what it meant to Tolkien, how it is wound into our own nature, and what it might mean to us now.

ELVİSH ΛESTHETİCS

'I desired dragons with a profound desire,' Tolkien tells us in his essay 'On Fairy-Stories'. The desire to see dragons and Elves is a not merely a desire to see a particular kind of exotic creature, he believes, but a desire for 'Faërie', a whole world, a 'realm or state' in which Elves and fairies and dragons have their being. If we really found a fire-breathing lizard in a zoo, that would be very boring: not what we are looking for at all. The other realm is desired precisely because it is 'imaginary'. It is desired because of something we find there, of which the very substance of that world is somehow composed. Some have called this 'magic', but (for reasons explained above) Tolkien prefers the word 'enchantment'. It is not an escape from reality.

> *Faërie* contains many things besides elves and fays, and besides dwarfs, witches, trolls, giants, or dragons: it holds the seas, the sun, the moon, the sky; and the earth, and all the things that are in it: tree and bird, water and stone, wine and bread, and ourselves, mortal men, when we are enchanted.

The secondary world of imagination is made, in fact, out of the primary world, and – this is the key point – it reveals or 'makes luminous' the things of which the primary world is made.

> By the forging of Gram cold iron was revealed; by the making of Pegasus horses were ennobled; in the Trees of the Sun and Moon root and stock, flower and fruit are manifested in glory.

Chesterton tells us in *Orthodoxy* that fairy-tales founded in him the conviction 'that this world is a wild and startling place, which might have been quite different, but which is quite delightful' (the 'feeling that something has been *done*', that every colour, every leaf, every creature is 'dramatic'). Similarly, Tolkien tells us that in fairy-tales he 'first divined the potency of the words, and the wonder of the things, such as stone, and wood, and iron; tree and grass; house and fire; bread and wine' ('On Fairy-Stories').

The realm of Faërie is an imaginary world, which is to say that it is made from images of real things as a pot is made of clay or a painting is made of paint. Yet we go there seeking a light that we cannot find in the primary world. The action of making or experiencing such a world is in part a creative act; we are in fact claiming our birthright to 'make by the law in which we're made' ; made, that is, 'in the image and likeness of a Maker'. The imaginal is where we sense most strongly the essence of creativity, of the divine imagination that conceives and gives life to the primary world. It is where words are born. It is the world where things could be other than they are, or not be at all, and where *what they are* is seen as for the first time, because it is seen against a background that looms much closer in Faërie: the background of pure light, or pure darkness.

With this in mind, let us read the description of Lothlórien as Frodo experiences it. It begins as follows, but is well worth going back to *The Lord of the Rings* to read it in full. I think it evokes an intense, almost mystical experience that lies close to the heart of the book.

> It seemed to him that he had stepped through a high window that looked on a vanished world. A light was upon it for which his language had no name. All that he saw was shapely, but the shapes seemed at once clear cut, as if they had been first conceived and drawn at the uncovering of his eyes, and ancient as if they had endured for ever.

Elvishness is a kind of beauty, then, or even the essence of all beauty. That does not mean that *only* Elves are beautiful, or that Hobbiton does not have a beauty of its own that differs from that of Rivendell or Lothlórien. Beauty is everywhere. But within earthly beauty, and more in some places and things than others, is a certain elusive quality that Tolkien tried to 'refine', if you like, within the figure of Elvishness.

It is a sense of freedom, of a yearned-for infinity. It is something like coming home, but only at the end of a long journey. In a word, I suppose, it is the glimpse of *transcendence*, of what it might mean to go beyond all limitation, outside time itself perhaps, into a place where beauty converges and commingles with goodness and truth.

The longing for transcendent beauty is associated with a sense of melancholy, of infinite distance or separation, because we are far from home. Tolkien associates this especially with starlight, with music, and with the sound of water. Elvish art is concerned mainly with memory, and therefore tends to be somewhat nostalgic or wistful. As time goes by, the Elves are increasingly filled with memory; when time comes to an end, memory is all they will have left. The tragedy of the Elves is that their yearning and love is for *this world*, which is passing away. Their existence is bound up with the created world which they contemplate, and with the 'sub-creativity' they exercise in accord with the gifts they have been given.

What Tolkien is ultimately concerned with is what he calls the 'ennoblement' of the human race, and we can see now that this must imply both a theory of sanctity and a theory of beauty. Elvishness when mingled with humanity 'ennobles' us because the Elves are our link back to the first Light, and their presence in our 'bloodstream' (i.e. as an element in our nature) enables us to recall the Light that shone in the eyes of those who lived in Valinor before ever the moon rose or the sun shone.

This light of 'art undivorced from reason' is the light of original participation. It is the light which bathed the world fresh from the hand of the Creator, when 'God saw that it was good'. A sensitivity to this light, or a memory of it, is what attracts us to the Elves. Without this yearning for the light, for the beautiful, it would never be possible for us to attain the new, more conscious participation or state of communion that Barfield and Tolkien both, in their different ways, anticipated. That state of communion, Tolkien believed, was finally attained and made possible in Christ, through the gift of the Holy Spirit. Unlike the art of the Elves, Christian art is consequently able to celebrate and express the overcoming of the infinite distance between heaven and earth. (The work of Fra Angelico, for example, is radiant with the glory of heaven shining through earthly forms.)[24]

Men seek in the future what Elves seek in the past. But the love of beauty, for what is first given and taken from us by time, is a necessary part of our nature, if we are to be able to receive the light when it returns, if we are to recognise the Author of our existence when 'the morning star rises in our hearts'. In that sense the infusion of an Elvish spirit into humanity means to Tolkien the awakening of a divine discontent, an *eros* for the transcendent, which Christianity must always presuppose and rely upon. Without it, our spirits could not be receptive: they would be hard and closed, where they should be liquid and open.

COMING HOME

'Elves, sir! I would dearly love to see *them*. Couldn't you take me to see Elves, sir, when you go?'

The thread of Elvishness is wound into human nature by the marriages of Beren and Lúthien, Tuor and Idril, Eärendil and Elwing. Finally the marriage of Aragorn and Arwen sets the scene for the Age of Men, in the later stages of which we are now living. In Minas Tirith the White Tree blooms again, and 'all the stars flowered in the sky'.

Tolkien's body lies beside his wife's in the graveyard at Wolvercote, just north of Oxford, under a stone marked at his request with the names of Beren and Lúthien. The romance of these great heroes of the First Age is a poetic visualisation of Tolkien's own spiritual and psychological autobiography, ending with a journey into the unknown world of death.

If the story of Beren and Lúthien was so important to Tolkien that he engraved it on his tomb, it seems likely that Beren and Lúthien were for him the primary 'archetypes' of Man and Elf respectively. The fact that one is male and the other female suggests that he placed in the Elves qualities that he associated very largely with women: delicacy, creativity, musicality, beauty, unfailing memory, profound wisdom, lasting fidelity. If this is true, the masculine-feminine dynamic that some critics have failed to find in Tolkien's work is central to the story and to the whole cycle of stories, though in a disguised fashion. It is explored through the historical relationships of Elves and Men, 'entwined' as they are through several key instances of intermarriage blessed by the gods. The love of beauty, which Tolkien symbolises as a love of Elves and of Faërie – and therefore, as he explains, a love of enchantment, of imagination, of creativity – is intimately related to the love that exists between man and woman. In Tolkien's own life this makes absolute sense, for his creative writing begins at the time of his love affair with Edith, and is deeply bound up with her and the children to whom he read so many of the stories.

We note also that for all the high epic poetry, the centre of *The Lord of the Rings* is not in Gondor, it is in the Shire, firmly rooted in the domestic. It is there that we must look for the final integration of Elvishness into human nature, within the romance as a whole. And this is what we find.

In one of his letters, Tolkien writes that the 'chief hero' of *The Lord of the Rings* is not Aragorn. It is not even Frodo. It is the unpretentious gardener, Sam Gamgee (L 131). Sam appears to the reader, at least at first, to be little more than a Sancho Panza to Frodo's Don Quixote. Yet precisely because Frodo is so elevated beyond the common life of the hobbits, it is Sam who is the truer incarnation of the Shire, and most deeply rooted in its soil. Sam's growth to maturity and the healing of the Shire go hand in hand. The story identifies this double process with Sam's winning of the hand of the girl he loves, and the book ends not with Aragorn's coronation, or with Frodo's departure into the West, but with his own return home to a loving wife and family.

> And he went on, and there was yellow light, and fire within; and the evening meal was ready, and he was expected. And Rose drew him in, and set him in his chair, and put little Elanor upon his lap.
>
> He drew a deep breath.
>
> 'Well, I'm back,' he said.

The story as a whole is concerned with 'the ennoblement (or sanctification) of the humble' (L 181). Sam is the humblest of hobbits, a servant without ambitions – except perhaps to see Elves and Oliphaunts, and eventually to have a bit of a garden of his own. For him to leave the Shire out of love for Frodo involves a great sacrifice. In a sense, he has to sacrifice the Shire itself – consciously so when he sees the threat to it in Galadriel's mirror but still determines to go on. It is fidelity to Frodo that remains his guiding star throughout. The plans of the Wise and the fate of Middle-earth are never his concern. He only knows he has to do his bit and help his master, however hopeless the task may seem. At a crucial moment in Mordor he must carry the Ring-bearer and even the Ring itself.

Sam moves from immature to mature innocence; and finally, back in his own sphere, the gardener and healer of gardens becomes a 'king' – or at least a mayor. In fact, the Appendices tells us that he was elected mayor of the Shire no less than seven times, and it is to him that King Elessar will entrust the Star of the Dúnedain, representing the crown of the North Kingdom.

Sam's strength is not in the 'ironmongery' he brings back from Gondor or his skill with a sword. It lies in the gift of healing that he bears from Galadriel: the box of blessed earth from her own orchard. Like Aragorn he has the power to heal his land of the hurts of war, and it is by this healing power that a true king is known, whether in Gondor or in Arnor. In Tolkien's intention, Sam is therefore paired with Aragorn as an 'heir of Elendil', the archetypal Elf-friend.

[101]

Aragorn is not the only great hero with whom Sam is paired, at a level just below the surface of the text. As they wait to be engulfed in the ruin of Mount Doom, Sam sighs to Frodo,

> 'What a tale we have been in, Mr Frodo, haven't we? I wish I could hear it told! Do you think they'll say: *Now comes the story of Nine-Fingered Frodo and the Ring of Doom*? And then everyone will hush, like we did, when in Rivendell they told us the tale of Beren One-Hand and the Great Jewel. I wish I could hear it! And I wonder how it will go on after our part.'

The reader is meant to identify Frodo with Beren, as Sam does. But an earlier exchange suggests a deeper intent on the author's part. After Gollum falls into the Fire, Sam catches sight of Frodo's bleeding hand.

> 'Your poor hand!' he said. 'And I have nothing to bind it with, or comfort it. I would have spared him a whole hand of mine rather. But he's gone now beyond recall, gone for ever.'

The desire to grasp is finally renounced; the grasping Shadow falls into the Fire and is forgiven. Frodo is marked by the loss of a finger – as Sauron lost a finger to Isildur – owing to his final (though in his case excusable) claiming of the Ring. Humble Sam may see Frodo as the great hero, but by that remark and the spirit it reveals it is Sam himself who is most closely conformed to Beren One-Hand – the great ancestor of Aragorn, and Tolkien's secret name for himself.

The story of Beren and Lúthien is echoed within *The Lord of the Rings* explicitly by the romance of Aragorn and Arwen. If I am right, it is echoed also by the long-postponed marriage of Samwise to Rosie Cotton, which represents the 'earthing' of the more distant epic marriages of Men and Elves. Of course, Rosie Cotton is not an Elven princess, any more than Tolkien's own Edith Bratt was. Nonetheless, it is a fact that when Sam names his first child (who, he says, takes after Rosie), he chooses to identify her with a flower that blooms only in Lothlórien. In *Sauron Defeated*, Christopher Tolkien tells us that his father's letter to Milton Waldman describing the projected Epilogue to *The Lord of the Rings* makes a point of referring to Elanor, 'who by a strange gift has the looks and beauty of an elven-maid; in her all [Sam's] love and longing for Elves is resolved and satisfied.'[25]

Perhaps most profoundly of all, this final comment shows that for Tolkien the male-female dynamic is not, finally, a matter of a couple only, uniting in harmony the human with the Elvish elements in our nature, but of a *fruitful* couple; that is to say, of a couple that is open to being blessed with new life. It is not simply with his marriage to Rosie that Sam's *eros* – his love and longing for Elves, the motivation for his journey – is fulfilled and blessed, but with the birth and growth within his home of Elanor and the other children.

THE HEALING OF ARDA

The Christian revelation does not enter explicitly into *The Lord of the Rings*. Tolkien reflected on many of the major themes that theologians are concerned with, but his thinking expressed itself there in imaginative mode – for the most part in the form of symbols and images. Yet the secondary world he created was set in the past of our world. This gave him the opportunity to connect it with the primary world in a more direct way, if he could do so without straining the conception to breaking point. That he attempted to do so is testimony to the seriousness with which he took his own project.

'The Debate of Finrod and Andreth' in the tenth volume of 'The History of Middle-Earth', which was at one time intended to form part of an Appendix to *The Silmarillion*, is probably the most theologically fascinating of all the posthumous works. It is also a powerful and emotionally moving piece of writing. Set in the First Age of the Sun before the meeting of Beren and Lúthien, the Debate takes place between an old wise-woman and Finrod, one of the brothers of Galadriel. It is accompanied by a detailed commentary and notes by Tolkien, which contain some of his most developed thinking about death and the soul, the relationship of Elves and Men, and the final destiny of both. We have already seen (in Chapter 4) that death is one of the major concerns in Tolkien's writing. Here is the most explicit treatment of the subject in his fiction.

The dialogue is intense and poignant, for a reason that we only discover at the end: that Andreth in her youth fell in love with one of Finrod's brothers, Aegnor. While Aegnor remains ever-young, and has departed from her, Andreth herself has faded and grown old. In attempting to console her in the course of their conversation, Finrod argues against Andreth's assumption that the aging and death of Men comes from Morgoth. He draws out from her the admission that in the distant past, Men may have committed some offence against the One God which led to the imposition of this penalty. Like all that comes from Eru, death would originally have been a beneficent gift, intended not for our hurt but for the perfection of our nature. Neither the body nor the death of the body were intended by him to be a burden, and nothing is evil in its beginning. (In line with Catholic teaching, Tolkien here is carefully countering any Gnostic or Manichaean tendency to view the physical body as an evil to be escaped or transcended.)

What he concludes is that the gift of death, which involves the separation of soul from body, was not intended to take this tragic form. Melkor's greatest success has been to turn it into an unnatural suffering, but in death before the Fall, rather than leaving it behind to rot, the soul of Man was to have taken the human body with it out of the whole realm of Arda, into eternity. This would have meant nothing less than a kind of *assumption into heaven*. The body would have been released from the limitations of time and space, and healed from all the damage Melkor had wrought since the beginning in the substances of Arda.

Tolkien's speculation has a long history behind it. The theologians of the Catholic Church have all agreed that the separation of body and soul in Man is an 'unnatural' state; that in some way the two components of human personality cannot be separated, and that they need each other. Since the most 'natural' human state is (by theological definition) that which existed before the Fall, some have asked themselves whether Adam and Eve would have died at all, if they had not eaten the forbidden fruit. The Book of Genesis tells us that after the original sin, God expels man from the garden lest he 'reach out his hand and take also from the tree of life, and eat, and live forever' (Gen. 3:22). This seems to imply that a tree of life had been placed in the garden for man to eat when the time was right, but that sin removed it beyond his reach. In other words, there was to have been a moment when death came to Man, but in that moment he would have eaten by God's permission from the tree of life. In the original plan, therefore, death would have occurred, but it would have taken a different form.

Melkor has turned death into a curse, but he has done more than that. By preventing the 'assumption' of the human body Finrod believes he may have prevented the salvation of the Elves too. Being immortal, they will eventually have to face the death of Arda, when time itself comes to an end. In the original plan of Eru, the assumption of the bodies of Men would have implied the creation of a 'new heavens and a new earth', an 'Arda Remade' in which the Elves, perhaps, might have dwelt with Men, their deliverers, in an eternal present flowing with endless bliss. Now, in 'Arda Marred' all seems to be forever lost.

Now Tolkien makes his boldest move yet. In the face of all the darkness he has painted, hovering on the edge of the darkest despair, through Finrod and Andreth he speaks to us of Hope (the 'little sister', as the poet Charles Péguy called her, of Faith and Love). Finrod's word for this kind of hope is *Estel*, meaning trust in our deepest nature and first being, despite the apparent contradiction of what is known and experienced. Prompted by this definition, the woman recalls that there are some of her kindred who call themselves People of the Old Hope. They prophesy 'that the One will himself enter into Arda, and heal Men and all the Marring from the beginning to the end.' For her part, she cannot see how such a thing could happen. Finrod, however, replies:

> 'If we are indeed the *Eruhin*, the Children of the One, then He will not suffer Himself to be deprived of His own, not by any Enemy, not even by ourselves. This is the last foundation of *Estel*, which we keep even when we contemplate the End: of all His designs the issue must be for His Children's joy.'

Not even by ourselves. That is bold indeed, and a mystery we cannot fathom even in prophecy, if it suggests that somehow God will save us even from our own evil will to reject his love, yet without doing violence to our freedom.

Christians believe that Eru, the Creator, has fulfilled the Old Hope of Andreth's people and done precisely what is needed to heal Arda from within. In the person of Jesus Christ he assumed human nature and suffered the worst Morgoth could throw at him. He allowed himself to be killed in the most violent way possible, experiencing the whole range of human suffering so that by filling it with his presence he could make it a bridge rather than a barrier between eternity and time. The fruit of that sacrifice can be seen already, the Church believes, in those most closely linked to Christ in time and space. The Virgin Mary, his mother, was assumed bodily into heaven at the moment of her death, just as (Tolkien suggests) Adam and Eve were intended to be in the beginning. In her the whole cosmos may find its way back to God. Perhaps the glory is greater now than it would have been, being won at such a cost. The hope of Arda is restored, and the Elves too may look forward with us to something 'more than memory'.

Tolkien was taking a great risk by inserting a prophecy of the Incarnation into his *legendarium*. Some readers may feel he has betrayed his principles, and that his religious beliefs are being allowed to intrude upon the story. Yet there is a great artistic integrity about the way it is done. Nothing is being forced: the characters are real within the secondary world, so much so that one feels great pity for Andreth and sympathy for Finrod. They do not step outside their own terms of reference within the secondary world.

What is happening here is that Tolkien is thinking through the Incarnation *from within his own subcreation*, almost as a way of testing its 'consistency' with reality. I believe it passes the test.

THE SECRET FIRE

Up to now, I have been speaking of light, and of beauty. Light is the life-blood of the world, of all things the most desirable, for it is the 'luminous form of the beautiful'.[26] It carries within itself the music of meaning. But the source of both light and beauty, according to Tolkien, is fire.

The 'secret fire' is Tolkien's term for the distinctive creative power of Eru. It is God's 'secret', for only God can truly create *ex nihilo* (from nothing). For Tolkien the fire represents life, love and creativity, the wisdom and love of God that burns at the heart of the world and sustains it in existence – it is a willed emanation from the creative energy of God's own self; it is the life of God shared with the world.

In Note 11 to the Commentary on the 'Debate' in *Morgoth's Ring* he writes that the Flame Imperishable 'appears to mean the Creative activity of Eru (in some sense distinct from or within Him), by which things could be given a "real" and independent (though derivative and created) existence.' It refers 'to the mystery of "authorship", by which the author, while remaining "outside" and independent of his work, also "indwells" in it, on its derivative plane, below that of his own being, as the source and guarantee of its being.'

In view of the earlier discussion, we might call it the divine *eros*. We normally associate God with love in the sense of *agape* or charity, and *eros* with the love of the sexes. But the word captures the passionate energy of God's love in a way that *agape* does not. The characteristic of *eros* is that it reaches out towards beauty: it is a response to beauty, or a recognition of it. In God's case it is the active *creation* of beauty. We find this wild, passionate, creative and fiery love of God enshrined in the very heart of the Bible as the Song of Songs.

Eru sends forth into the void 'the Flame Imperishable' to be the heart of the world. He has kindled the Ainur into reality with the same fire. This fire is that which Melkor seeks in the void, hoping to use it to create beings of his own, but he does not find it, 'for it is with Ilúvatar'. Thus it is that the Enemy cannot make, but only mar. He can imitate, distort and copy, he can mock and corrupt, but he cannot truly create. Yet all his desire is bent on creation, and his inner torment is caused by this eternal frustration. He has become a flame, but a flame that gives more heat than light. He burns, which is to say he consumes instead of illuminating. His fire, compared to that of Eru/Ilúvatar, is shadow.

The ambiguity of the symbol 'fire' comes into play in the following passage:

> The Balrog reached the bridge. Gandalf stood in the middle of the span, leaning on the staff in his left hand, but in his other hand Glamdring gleamed, cold and white . . .
>
> 'You cannot pass,' he said. The orcs stood still, and a dead silence fell. 'I am a servant of the Secret Fire, wielder of the flame of Anor. You cannot pass. The dark fire will not avail you, flame of Udûn. Go back to the Shadow! You cannot pass.'[27]

The fire that is of God burns without consuming. Lesser fires may give light, and they may be used to give life and form to other creatures, but at the same time they consume the fuel on which they depend. Thus all lesser fires depend on God's gift of being, of fuel, of substance, continually renewed. The Enemy wishes not to depend on God, not to receive from him, but instead to be self-sufficient. That is not possible. Even the Balrog owes his existence not to Melkor, but to Ilúvatar.

The Book of Wisdom describes something that appears very similar to Tolkien's 'secret fire'. Wisdom or *Sophia* is said to precede the creation of the world and to be placed at its very heart: 'For she is a breath of the power of God, and a pure emanation of the glory of the Almighty: therefore nothing defiled gains entrance into her. For she is a reflection of eternal light: a spotless mirror of the working of God, and an image of his goodness' (Wisdom 7:25–6).[28]

Other biblical references to the secret fire are not hard to find. Adam and Eve are said to have been prevented from returning to the Garden of Eden by a 'fiery sword'. The Lord appears to Abraham like a fire walking between the divided animals when he makes the great Covenant with him and his descendants. The Prophet Elijah calls down fire from heaven to consume a sacrifice soaked in water, when he restores the religion of Israel. Moses encounters God in the burning bush when he is told to lead the people out of Egypt. Later, after talking with God on the mountain, the face of Moses shines so brightly that it has to be veiled. He tells the people: 'The Lord your God is a consuming fire. . .' (Deut. 4:24). We see at the end of the Book of Exodus that God dwells in a luminous cloud, the manifestation of divine glory, which appears within the Tent that serves the Israelites as a Temple.

The New Testament – and the tradition of theological reflection based upon it – refines our understanding of the inner life of God yet further, for the Incarnation reveals God to be a Trinity of persons. And in Christian tradition it is the third person who is particularly identified with fire, for the Holy Spirit descends on the Apostles at Pentecost like 'tongues of flame'. Jesus tells his disciples, 'I came to bring fire to the earth, and how I wish it were already kindled! I have a baptism with which to be baptised, and what stress I am under until it is completed!' (Luke 12:49)

In the New Testament, the secret fire is revealed to be not merely a force or a power, but a person in his own right. The Spirit is the personified Love that burns between the Father and Son, the Love that gives life and grace. No wonder Melkor sought it, and no wonder it could not be found, for it can be known only by those to whom it is given.

God dwells in 'light inaccessible', yet in the New Testament that light emanates from and rests upon a living man. Peter, James and John see their master clothed in this light and transfigured by it on Mount Tabor. 'I am the light of the world,' he tells the man born blind (John 9:5). It is the Incarnation which takes away the veil.

> Now the Lord is the Spirit, and where the Spirit of the Lord is, there is freedom. And all of us, with unveiled faces, seeing the glory of the Lord as though reflected in a mirror, are being transformed into the same image from one degree of glory to another; for this comes from the Lord, the Spirit (2 Cor. 3:17–18).

The person who has seen the Son has seen the Father, and whoever has seen the Son has also seen the Holy Spirit. The eyes of faith become 'eyes of fire', which see by virtue of a likeness to what is seen. The unity and distinction of the persons in God compose the secret of Christian sanctity, for we are called to personal unity in Christ, in which our own truest identity and mission will be revealed.

St Bonaventure writes of the ecstasy of contemplation, experienced by those who have followed the 'mind's journey into God': 'This is mystical and most secret, which no one knows except him who receives it, no one receives except him who desires it, and no one desires except him who is penetrated to the marrow by the fire of the Holy Spirit, whom Christ sent into the world.'

In the history of the Church we often find particular sanctity associated with a visible radiance, and even with flames. People rushed to put out a blaze in the forest of Umbria, to find nothing but St Francis and St Clare talking together. The light of the Transfiguration shining from St Seraphim of Sarov in 1831 also filled a forest glade. St Philip Neri, was praying in the catacombs of Rome when a great ball of fire descended into his chest. From that day onwards he emanated a warm glow even in winter, on which people could warm their hands, and when he died it was found that his heart had been strangely enlarged, displacing two of his ribs.

Tolkien shows us how to 'think' with the imagination, using concrete images. Christianity, too, cannot dispense with *mythopoeia*. Theologians may speculate endlessly about the 'divine energies' and whether these are notionally or really distinct from the divine essence, or about the act of Being (*esse*) and how it is participated by the world, or about the Holy Spirit and how he unites us in love with the Blessed Trinity, but in the end it is more important to kneel in adoration before an image of the Sacred Heart crowned with flames, or the Eucharist itself blazing out from the hands of the priest.

All love, all hope, all music finds a home with God, 'who with divine freedom, but also with divine consistency, has fashioned for himself in his creation a body through which to reveal his glory.'[29] Here in this body is the secret fire of our making and of our re-making, the luminous centre of a new universe.

CONCLUSION:
TOLKIEN'S ACHIEVEMENT

> Do not laugh! But once upon a time (my crest has long since fallen) I had a mind to make a body of more or less connected legend, ranging from the large and cosmogonic, to the level of romantic fairy-story – the larger founded on the lesser in contact with the earth, the lesser drawing splendour from the vast backcloths – which I could dedicate simply to: to England; to my country. . . . The cycles should be linked to a majestic whole, and yet leave scope for other minds and hands, wielding paint and music and drama. Absurd.
>
> *J. R. R. Tolkien to Milton Waldeman (L 131)*

Absurd indeed. But we are not laughing. Tolkien, not alone, perhaps, but with the help of his son, achieved what he dreamed of achieving. The above extract is from a letter to a publisher in 1951 that was originally 10,000 words long and is not reproduced in full even in the published collection. The publication of *The Lord of the Rings* was hanging in the balance, and the letter was an attempt to show that it needed to appear together with *The Silmarillion*.

As we have already seen, Tolkien goes on to explain that the stories came first, growing in his mind as 'given' things: 'always I had the sense of recording what was already "there", somewhere: not of "inventing"'. *The Hobbit* was originally unrelated: he did not know at first that it belonged to the cycle.

> But it proved to be the discovery of the completion of the whole, its mode of descent to earth, and merging into 'history'.

Thus *The Lord of the Rings* and *The Silmarillion*, expanded now to include a host of other stories and fragments in 'The History of Middle-Earth', provide us with an immense mythological tapestry woven of many threads, taken from the legends of Northern Europe and elsewhere. The connection with 'England' remains, though not in the way he had earlier envisaged.

We know from 'The History of Middle-Earth', particularly *The Book of Lost Tales* (pre-1920), that his mythology was in part an attempt to explain the 'Elvishness' of England. The great city of Avallónë (Avalon, which of course enters into the tales of Arthur) stands on the coast of the Lonely Isle (Tol Eressëa), an island like a great ship, on which Ulmo drew the Elves across the sea, anchoring it eventually near the coast of Aman. In Tolkien's original conception this was to have been England itself, before it was invaded and disfigured by Men. The Elvish city of Kortirion was none other than Warwick (where Tolkien and Edith were married). The wistful atmosphere of the early Tales is concentrated in a couple of important and rather beautiful poems: *The Cottage of Lost Play* and *Kortirion among the Trees*. But as time went by, in Tolkien's imagination England moved eastwards (to somewhere in Beleriand and perhaps later Eriador), while the Lonely Isle floated westwards. The Undying Lands retreated before him, becoming ever more remote, eventually being removed from the earth completely.

The direct 'historical' links between England and Elvendom may have become tenuous, but in another way, as I have tried to show throughout this book, Tolkien succeeded in uncovering the Elvishness he had sensed buried deep within the languages and folklore of England, and expressed this in a mythological creation of enormous subtlety, power and versatility.

It is often assumed by Christians that when God became Man, he fulfilled the ancient prophecies and thereby made all mythology redundant. Henceforth all mythological thinking would be something of a relapse back into superstition and ignorance. The sun had risen; the shadows were banished. But Tolkien is saying something different. A sun that does not cast shadows in broad daylight would be no sun at all. In the Epilogue to his essay 'On Fairy-Stories' he writes:

> Redeemed Man is still man. Story, fantasy, still go on, and should go on. The Evangelium has not abrogated legends; it has hallowed them, especially the 'happy ending'. The Christian still has to work, with mind as well as body, to suffer, hope, and die; but he may now perceive that all his bents and faculties have a purpose, which can be redeemed. So great is the bounty wit which he has been treated that he may now, perhaps, fairly dare to guess that in Fantasy he may actually assist in the effoliation and multiple enrichment of creation.

Tolkien thus stands with the rest of the Inklings and those who believe that Christianity does not abolish *mythopoeia* or poetic knowledge, but makes possible a new era of 'baptised mythology', mythology that is no longer religion but 'fairy-tale', an indispensable poetic evocation of a great mystery that is still unfolding within the world. 'Art has been verified. God is the Lord, of angels, and of men – and of elves. Legend and history have met and fused.' Christ may have come, but 'the end is not yet'. When it does come, even then there will be no end to the making of stories and of music.

The highest function of the fairy-tale, Tolkien tells us, is found in the sudden miraculous 'turn', the grace of deliverance, the *eucatastrophe* or happy ending. This is not escapist, because it does not deny sorrow and failure, and indeed 'the possibility of these is necessary to the joy of deliverance'. But it denies *universal or final* defeat, by giving a taste or echo of victory, the final victory of Eru, who incorporates with his infinite creativity and foresight even evil into his design. Evil does not cease to be evil, and must never be deliberately chosen; but it can never conquer the Good, which shines more brightly the more it is engulfed in darkness.

> It is the mark of the good fairy-story, of the higher or more complete kind, that however wild its events, however fantastic or terrible the adventures, it can give to the child or man that hears it, when the 'turn' comes, a catch of the breath, a beat and lifting of the heart, near to (or accompanied by) tears, as keen as that given by any form of literary art, and having a peculiar quality.

This 'turn' cannot be produced by doctrinal statement alone, no matter how true this is. It cannot be evoked in this way, because it essentially involves a moment of perception, which as we have seen is imaginative perception, or a seeing beyond the surface of things into their ultimate meaning. It is evoked by poetry that comes fresh from experience, rather than the kind of prose which delivers experience at second-hand. (That is why when Julian of Norwich says to us 'All will be well, and every kind of thing will be well', we are moved to believe in a way that we are not when confronted by a more banal statement, such as, 'Don't worry, everything will be OK.')

'There is a place called "heaven" where the good here unfinished is completed; and where the stories yet unwritten, and the hopes unfulfilled, are continued' (L 45). The stories that we have received from Tolkien through his son are incomplete, and no doubt themselves only a pale and imperfect shadow of what he was striving to bring into the world. We may hope to see and hear them completed by the author in Arda Healed. Nevertheless, even as they stand, Tolkien's tree of tales forms a worthy enough backdrop to the one true fairy-tale, which is the tale of the Incarnation. For those who, despite having heard the word 'Christianity', have never been introduced to the Gospel in a way that makes sense to them (or indeed, that does anything other than depress them!), reading Tolkien may be a revelation in itself. It may enable them to 'hear' that Gospel as if for the first time, as the earth-shattering surprise it truly is – a surprise even to the gods who made the music before time.

In this book I have explored some of the reasons why Tolkien is one of the great spiritual writers of our time – of the age which dawned in the trenches of the First World War, and today finds the shadows lengthening with the war on terrorism. He explored the human meaning of loss and death; which is what gives heroism, whether Christian or Pagan, its poignancy. The symbolic and interior struggle of Good with Evil, of virtue against temptation and weakness, of tradition against corruption and treachery, are represented realistically enough in the *legendarium* for us to be justified in seeing these works as a vehicle of great wisdom born of experience and suffering.

For Tolkien *did* suffer, as all do who live in such times, both personally and vicariously through a sensitivity to others. He was a man of his times, a product of modernity; yet at the same time, through faith, hope and love, he transcended his times. His writing is dark – darker than his critics realise – yet it is suffused with the hope (*Estel*) that we need to find in ourselves if we are to carry on without turning back.

> 'The brave things in the old tales and songs, Mr Frodo: adventures, as I used to call them. I used to think that they were things the wonderful folk of the stories went out and looked for, because they wanted them, because they were exciting and life was a bit dull, a kind of sport, as you might say. But that's not the way of it with the tales that really mattered, or the ones that stay in the mind. Folk seem to have been just landed in them, usually – their paths were laid that way, as you put it. But I expect they had lots of chances, like us, of turning back, only they didn't.'

Sam first enters the tale by his ears, as Gandalf hoists him through the window at Bag End and 'punishes' him for eavesdropping on the story of the Ring by sending him to Mordor with Frodo. Like Sam, we enter the story by listening, fascinated, to the Tale of the Ring. We find, like him, that once we are inside such a tale, it is difficult to escape, for our lives have been changed. We know the peril that threatens us, a darkness which encompasses the light. We realise that we are called to some form of service, so that the light may not perish from the earth. It is our knowledge of a light and a beauty worth defending that inspires heroism – even the heroism of hobbits, who are inspired to risk their lives by their love of the homely beauty of the Shire.

And it is the glimpse of a light and beauty that in a sense does not need defending which consoles the hero in his quest, and brings him peace of heart in the midst of his struggle. Deep within Mordor, looking up at the sky,

> Sam saw a white star twinkle for a while. The beauty of it smote his heart, as he looked up out of the forsaken land, and hope returned to him. For like a shaft, clear and cold, the thought pierced him that in the end the Shadow was only a small and passing thing: there was light and high beauty for ever beyond its reach.

It is the glimpse of high Elvish beauty that inspires heroism, whether in the Third Age or this, the Seventh Age of the Sun.

APPEПDİCES

An Archetypal Journey: Tolkien and Jung

We have seen that the quest of the Ring is presented from the start as a spiritual process that must be gone through, as much as it is a physical journey through hardship and danger. C. G. Jung's description of the therapeutic journey of the self can be helpful in describing some aspects of this process.

> There is in every word set down by the imaginative mind an awful under-current of meaning, and evidence and shadow upon it of the deep places out of which it has come. It is often obscure, often half-told . . . but, if we choose to dwell upon it and trace it, it will lead us always securely back to that metropolis of the soul's dominion' (John Ruskin).[30]

Timothy R. O'Neill's *The Individuated Hobbit* begins by giving an account of the rough outlines of Jung's theory, which, like Barfield's is concerned with the evolution of consciousness. For Jung the psyche is divided between the personal conscious, the personal unconscious and the collective unconscious. The latter is the repository of primordial images and predispositions termed archetypes, resembling the beds of rivers where the waters of life and common experience have dug deep channels. These archetypes, more or less charged with the psychic energy (*numen*) flowing through them, may reveal themselves and emerge into consciousness in the form of symbols, whether in dream or myth.

For Jung, the central archetypes are located in the strata of the psyche: consciousness is centred on an archetype called the *ego*, which acts as its controlling force under cover of the *persona* or social façade. The archetype of the persona, however, excludes all those emotions and images felt to be incompatible with civilised existence. These cluster around a deeper complex, below the level of consciousness, termed the *shadow*. This is a

[119]

personification of the dark side of our nature. Depending on whether the individual is male or female, there will also be a series of repressed or undeveloped masculine and feminine characteristics (the ones our ego has less use for). These cluster around another deep archetype called the *animus* or *anima*. And hidden more deeply still is the archetype of the *self*, which forms a potential alternative centre of the psyche as a whole, capable of integrating and unifying its various energies, and healing the fractures and imbalances between the various components.

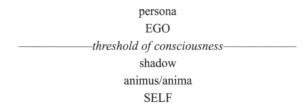

persona

EGO

————————*threshold of consciousness*————————

shadow

animus/anima

SELF

Most of us are damaged and in need of healing. This can be accomplished by a process termed 'individuation' by Jung. To put it crudely, the Self must be brought out of the depths and assume the position currently occupied by the ego. In fairy-tales, this process is often represented as a search for buried or captured treasure, and its retrieval through perils and darkness as the hero brings it through the shadow into the full light of consciousness.

> Our motivation is directed toward the ultimate joining of conscious and unconscious, and to the emergence of the Self as the new centre of a balanced psyche. This is the final achievement to which these archetypal urges direct us. The Trickster in fairy tales may provide us with elusive clues; the Wise Old Man, archetype of wisdom and power, may guide us; the redeemer may sacrifice himself for the quest. Without the final goal of Self-realization, the symbols are only curiosities'.[31]

A Jungian reads *The Lord of the Rings* as an account of 'the individuation of the West'. The real goal of the quest, according to O'Neill (pp. 50–51), is to heal the neurosis represented by the sinking of Númenor and the subsequent decay of its colonies in Middle-earth. O'Neill regards the very name that Tolkien has given to Atlantis in his mythos as being more than coincidentally related to Jung's term for psychic energy. 'With the loss of Númenor the psyche of the West is suddenly unbalanced, the fleeting selfhood of that golden age lost beneath the waves (in the depths of the unconscious).'

The White Tree is one of the archetypes of the life process – the flow of *numen*.

> The withering of the tree is symptomatic of the centuries of decay and grief in Gondor, culminating in the death of the last king of the line of Anárion. In the veins of the King is the blood of the Lords of Númenor, the blood of Eärendil and Elwing, in which the opposites [Elves and Men] are united (p. 50).

Thus the eventual 'Return of the King' (who has been preserved in hope by the Dúnedain, the broken sword his symbol) is the return of the Self of the West as an integrating force. The Shire is Middle-earth in microcosm, so the Scouring of the Shire is a version of the same process of individuation in 'Hobbit-mode', as it were.

Transformation always comes at a price. The healing of the soul of the West can only come about through facing, integrating and dissolving the shadow, so that the Self can emerge into the light of consciousness. Sauron is the shadow of Middle-earth, and of Aragorn as the true King. Gollum is the shadow of the hobbits: of Bilbo, Frodo and Sam. Despised and outcast, he personifies the potential moral weakness and evil that lurks in the soul of the most humble. Sam frequently advises Frodo to kill him when he has the chance, and the hatred between them is one of the themes of their journey into the Land of Shadow.

There is probably a connection between the vulnerability of Sam to that hatred for a hobbit long ago corrupted by the Ring, and the evident vulnerability of the Shire to the corruption brought upon it by Saruman during the War of the Ring. The corruption of the Shire is made possible by the collaboration of a certain number of the hobbits themselves with the rule of the ruffians. Hobbiton can only be healed of this moral weakness by the reordering of the Hobbit soul; and Sam's soul is reordered and healed at the very end of the quest, on the side of Mount Doom, by first sparing and finally forgiving Gollum. The death of Gollum represents the facing and overcoming of the shadow both within and without.

It is easy to recognise Jungian archetypes in many of the other characters and symbols introduced by Tolkien into his narrative. Gandalf, pretty obviously, is the 'wise old man' who features as guide to the psyche in the process of individuation. His staff is a traditional symbol of this hermeneutic function: linking heaven and earth. In some mythologies it carries a serpent or tamed dragon, which in Gandalf's case is suggested by the fire that it can produce at his command, and by its association with the conquest of Smaug in the earlier adventure. He is also a personification of the emerging Self of the West: his 'greyness' purged in a confrontation with his 'shadow' (the Balrog), he appears as Gandalf the White, the head of his Order. Aragorn, too, must pass through the shadow before he achieves mastery: he chooses the Paths of the Dead, and leads the unresolved elements in the unconscious of the West (the dead Oath-Breakers) to a final act of expiation.

Galadriel features in the Jungian reading of *The Lord of the Rings* as a powerful positive symbol of the feminine archetype, and Shelob as the negative feminine within the Land of Shadow. Eowyn is another powerful female figure. The Jungian writer Helen Luke once described the King of the Ringwraiths accurately enough as 'the ghost-like horror of the masculine spirit turned daemonic'. That despair-inducing horror can only be slain by Eowyn as woman, and she must strike at its head, for it has no heart. She confronts the Ringwraith over the body of her fallen king, Théoden, representing chivalry and the old heroic virtues, which cannot avail against the Nazgûl. Eowyn strikes with the power of the heart, of personal devotion, of womanhood, assisted of course by Merry, the 'child' that she as woman nurtures and protects.

The potential weakness of a Jungian interpretation of *The Lord of the Rings* emerges to view when O'Neill identifies the Ring of Power with the Jungian 'Self' – surely almost an inversion of its true meaning. Concentrating on its perfect circular shape and colour, he sees it as a positive image when Tolkien obviously intends the opposite. Tolkien's Ring suggests the power of the Enemy to deceive and to tempt. 'All that is gold does not glitter', as the rhyme says of Aragorn; the Ring is not the Self but the false self, the self that binds and does not liberate. For O'Neill, Frodo's loss of the Ring explains why his own healing, his own self-realisation, is precluded at the end of the book. Yet it is hard to see what Frodo could have done with the Ring that would not have turned him into another shadow.

The greatest flaw in the Jungian position from a Christian standpoint, and certainly from Tolkien's, is to regard God as what O'Neill calls 'an image projected by the psyche'. This leads him to omit the moral dimensions of the quest. Spirit transcends psyche: the Christian understanding of our moral life depends upon this distinction being made correctly. Morality is more than psychodynamics.

Jacques Maritain writes about the relationship of the unconscious and the spirit in his *Creative Intuition*:

> Reason does not only consist of its conscious logical tools and man-ifestations, nor does the will consist only of its deliberate conscious determinations. Far beneath the sunlit surface thronged with explicit concepts and judgments, words and expressed resolutions or move-ments of the will, are the sources of knowledge and creativity, of love and supra-sensuous desires, hidden in the primordial translucid night of the intimate vitality of the soul. Thus it is that we must recognise the existence of an unconscious or preconscious which pertains to the spiritual powers of the human soul and to the inner abyss of personal freedom, and of the personal thirst and striving for knowing and seeing, grasping and expressing: a spiritual or musical unconscious which is specifically different from the automatic or deaf unconscious.'[32]

By referring to the 'deaf' unconscious, Maritain means the Freudian unconscious, which consists of instinct and memory, complexes and repressed emotions. It is called 'deaf' because it is unreceptive to the intel-lect. The spiritual or musical unconscious, on the other hand, is the seed-bed of poetic knowledge and creative intuition. The distinction that Freud's dis-ciple Jung made between the personal and the collective unconscious, according to Maritain, is something quite different again, which cuts across both. Each of Jung's two constructs may be part of Maritain's spiritual or his automatic unconscious, depending on whether they are considered to be turned towards the world of the spirit or the world of matter, the intellect or the animal in us. We need both, for we human beings are not angels or entirely material creatures.

Although Tolkien would not have put it this way, a purely psychological account of man ignores a vital dimension of our existence, namely that in which we are able (with the help of divine grace) to transcend our biological and even psychological existence. This process – termed in the Christian tradition not individuation but divinisation – involves an additional discernment, not just between the ego and the Self but between the Self and the false self. This path is not one of balancing the elements and forces of the psyche alone, for at the level of the spirit we are part of a greater whole even than that of the Self. The false self can only be distinguished once the Self has been found, and at that point we are powerless to achieve the quest without help that comes from beyond ourselves.

Tolkien's Social Philosophy

The Shire has been described by critics as an 'agrarian idyll', an impossible paradise based on childhood memories, bathed in the rosy glow of sentimental nostalgia. This is not at all fair. Even before its infiltration and corruption by Saruman, the Shire has its flaws. The small-mindedness of its inhabitants, the unpleasantness of the Sackville-Bagginses and Ted Sandyman, are not there merely for comic effect, but inject a genuine note of realism from the primary world.

In 1943 Tolkien wrote: 'My political opinions lean more and more to Anarchy (philosophically understood, meaning abolition of control not whiskered men with bombs) – or to "unconstitutional" Monarchy' (L 52). Nor does he have much truck with the modern notion of the nation state: 'I would arrest anybody who uses the word State (in any sense other than the inanimate realm of England and its inhabitants, a thing that has neither power, rights nor mind); and after a chance of recantation, execute them if they remained obstinate!' Government, he adds, 'is an abstract noun meaning the art and process of governing and it should be an offence to write it with a capital G or so as to refer to people.'

The 'half republic half aristocracy' of the Shire (L 183) has an elected mayor but seems to function most of the time well enough without government, and its police force of 'Shirriffs' has very little to do – that is, until Saruman's influence is brought to bear. At that point Government with a capital G arrives with a vengeance. No political system as such is immune to corruption. 'I am *not* a 'democrat', Tolkien wrote in 1956,

> only because 'humility' and equality are spiritual principles corrupted by the attempt to mechanise and formalise them, with the

result that we get not universal smallness and humility, but universal greatness and pride, till some Orc gets hold of a ring of power – and then we get and are getting slavery' (L 186).

Tolkien was not optimistic about the prospects for a civilisation that had taken the path of Saruman rather than that of Gandalf (see L 53).

These real-life political opinions, which lie behind his fictionalised portrayal of English country life in the Shire, place Tolkien within a tradition of Catholic social thought known as 'Distributism', whose most eloquent exponents in the previous generation were Hilaire Belloc and Gilbert Keith Chesterton. As far as I know, he never referred to the Distributists, or aligned himself with their cause. Nevertheless, before the Second World War Distributism had been one of the two main Catholic movements in Britain basing itself upon the social teaching of the Church. Tolkien tended to avoid politics where he could, and refers to Chesterton mainly as a poet. Nevertheless, I cannot see any political 'camp' that would have suited him better. He was certainly no 'socialist' in any sense (see L 181). The other popular Catholic movement, the Catholic Social Guild, would have been more congenial to him, but after 1942 it was increasingly aligned with the Labour Party. In any case, Tolkien's work and interests lay elsewhere.

Distributists saw the family as the only solid basis for civil society and of any sustainable civilisation. They believed in a society of households, and were suspicious of top-down government. Power, they held, should be devolved to the lowest level compatible with a reasonable degree of order (the principle of 'subsidiarity'). Social order flows from the natural bonds of friendship, co-operation and family loyalty, within the context of a local culture possessing a strong sense of right and wrong. It cannot be imposed by force, and indeed force should never be employed except as a last resort and in self-defence.

The problem with modern Capitalism, in the opinion of the Distributists, was that there were not enough capitalists around: property and wealth had become concentrated in the hands of a few, reducing other people to the status of 'wage slaves' (hence the title of Belloc's book on the subject, *The Servile State*). The result in Britain had been a pseudo-democracy which was really a disguised plutocracy: actual power lay with the employers and the managers, and political parties were largely being manipulated by these for their own ends, public opinion being handled by allied interests in the media.

Distributists thought the answer lay in the direction of wider ownership (*not* 'public ownership'); meaning that measures should be taken to encourage small and family-run businesses, farmers and local retailers, and to defend them against the larger conglomerates. Forcible redistribution of land, however – of the kind we have seen recently in Zimbabwe – was not an option: it was completely against Distributist principles. One of the most basic of these principles was freedom: the whole point of the philosophy was to foster self-sufficiency, independence and personal responsibility.

The Shire fits neatly into this tradition of social thought. It represents an agricultural, largely self-sufficient way of life, cut off from the rest of the world and happy to remain so, that was already almost dead in Tolkien's time, killed by new methods of transport and communication. It was a way of life founded on local tradition, which Chesterton once famously called 'the democracy of the dead' – one shaped by our ancestors, not just by those who happened to be walking around. More importantly, perhaps, it was founded on a respect for nature and for the environment that we seem to have lost in the headlong rush for economic growth at all costs.

The Shadow of King Arthur

When the Israelites first demanded a king, Samuel told them in no uncertain words what they could expect.

> 'These will be the ways of the king who will reign over you: he will take your sons and appoint them to his chariots and to be his horsemen, and to run before his chariots . . . He will take the best of your fields and vineyards and olive orchards and give them to his servants . . . He will take the tenth of your flocks, and you shall be his slaves. And in that day you will cry out because of your king, whom you have chosen for yourselves; but the Lord will not answer you in that day (1 Sam. 8:11–18).

The Lord told Samuel, 'they have rejected me from being king over them' (1 Sam. 8:7).

Kingship is arguably the source of our most potent political mythology. The Israelites were not to be dissuaded from their decision 'to be like other nations'. And we find all that Samuel prophesied coming true. Yet God brings good out of evil, and in King David, only a generation later, he raises up a true hero: a king who is also a prophet, a poet and a liberator. Builder-up of the great city Jerusalem, David is also a sinner. The privilege of creating a temple for the Lord is consequently reserved for his son Solomon – whose very name has become synonymous with wisdom, and the splendour of whose reign is legendary. 'The king made silver as common in Jerusalem as stones, and he made cedars as numerous as the sycamores of the Shephelah' (1 Kings 10:27). Yet Solomon, too, fell, and lower than his father ever did – with hundreds of women and foreign gods – until the Lord raised up enemies against him.

Each great king is able – or at least attempts – to draw on the mystique already accumulated around the names of his predecessors. We see it in the Caesars; we see it in those who would imitate them: Charlemagne, Napoleon, Hitler. We see it in the tsars and kings and princes of every country and region. In England we see it expressed in the legends of Arthur and the histories of Alfred; we see William the Conqueror, Richard the Lionheart, Henry VIII and Elizabeth I aspiring to the same mantle, with varying degrees of success. The abuses of kingship are notorious. Yet even now (in some parts of the world) the institution survives. Americans often fail to understand its appeal – except in terms of the glamour that attaches to great entertainers like Elvis, or great political soap opera stars like the members of the Kennedy clan.

In keeping with the origins of their nation, the more archetypally American the hero, the more he (or she) is a lone individual set against a system or a wilderness. Even the five-minute heroes of the screen draw upon that mystique. Yet having a Royal Family at least enshrines the principle that society revolves around the family and not the individual.

G. K. Chesterton's *Ballad of the White Horse*, which Tolkien knew, is largely about the romance of kingship, in those far-off days when a king could be at the same time a hero. Such a king is not merely a lone individual, but the representative and guardian of a realm and a people, whether by virtue of the Blood Royal or by divine appointment (like Saul and David). Nevertheless, the hero, even when he is a king, must always be more than a cipher or a figurehead. The power of the archetype comes into its own when the king manages to combine possession of the cardinal virtues with the opportunity to act decisively at one of the turning points of history. Then archetype can serve personality, and personality the archetype: the king is worthy of the honour he receives. Such a monarch can become for each of us a living symbol not only of what binds us together in society, but of what we each aspire to become in our own circle.

Every nation has a legend or set of legends that help to define and enshrine its sense of identity and mission. For Chesterton, whose thought is so close to that of Tolkien in these matters, a national identity is shaped by the interplay of legend with landscape. Countries become beautiful, he thinks, by being loved – by being transformed in love by the imagination of those who live and die there. Those who have lived become part of the landscape and part of the legend. Graves and monuments are for visiting, and the shrine at the end of a pilgrimage provides a meeting place between earth and heaven that sanctifies the whole realm.

For Romantics such as Chesterton and Tolkien, imagination is an organ of perception, not merely of fancy. Mythology may be the only way that certain truths can find expression. But the imagination can also transmit a lie, a false perception. Tolkien writes of the way Hitler had corrupted the imagination of Europe: 'Ruining, perverting, misapplying, and making for ever accursed, that noble northern spirit, a supreme contribution to Europe, which I have ever loved, and tried to present in its true light' (L 45). The dark side of the imagination is to provide the irrational basis for all kinds of injustice and cruelty. In a fallen and corrupted world, our imagination is in desperate need of healing. It may still be an organ of perception, but the inner senses have light only through the moral organs of the soul.

The national legend of England was given form in the high Middle Ages by Geoffrey of Monmouth, Robert de Borron, the Cistercians, Malory and a host of lesser storytellers. The whole edifice of Arthurian legend was based on fragmentary historical tales of a great chieftain who defended the remains of the Imperium from the barbarians after the protection of Rome was withdrawn. The Kingdom of Logres is, of course, more than a part (or even the whole) of what we now call Britain. It is our *inner kingdom*. Overthrown by human sin and weakness as soon as it was glimpsed on the stage of history, it was not destroyed but 'withdrawn' into the imaginal landscape of Britain, just as Arthur himself was not killed on the field by Mordred but transported to the Island of Avalon.

Avalon itself is often identified with Glastonbury Tor, which other legends link to the visit of St Joseph of Arimathea with the Holy Grail. Joseph himself is symbolically linked by his cup and flowering staff to the two other Josephs of the Bible, in the Old and the New Testaments respectively. The national legend of England is thus a thoroughly 'Christian' legend (in fact a bit too obvious a Christian allegory, Tolkien thought). Arthur's perennial mission is to render England receptive to the Blood of Christ, a receptivity of which the Grail is the emblem, and the flowering staff the result. (In the film *Excalibur*, the land literally blossoms under the hooves of Arthur's knights.)

The Arthur story, like all Christian myths, conforms itself to its own supreme archetype, the story of Christ which is both myth and history. Just as Christ gathered his twelve disciples, so Arthur gathered his knights. As the Logos died on the cross before his kingdom could be realised on earth, so Logres ended in a field of blood and betrayal. But the perennial hope of healing and resurrection lives in the Grail, in the Eucharist, which may always be revealed to those who search for it. And as Christ will come again, so in him Arthur will one day restore the Kingdom of Logres.

Myths Transformed

After the publication of *The Lord of the Rings*, Tolkien became increasingly self-conscious about the work. Frequently he would have to explain it to the many admirers who wrote to him, and when doing so he tried to fill in details left vague or implicit in the published writings. By the end of the 1950s, his son writes, when he turned back to the Silmarillion papers, he realised he now had to 'satisfy the requirements of a coherent theological and metaphysical system, rendered now more complex in its presentation by the supposition of obscure and conflicting elements in its roots and tradition'. (I am quoting throughout this section from the part of *Morgoth's Ring* called 'Myths Transformed'.)

In particular, his respect for astronomy had led him to doubt his own mythological conception of a flat earth becoming round after the Fall of Númenor, and populated well before the coming of the sun. He began to feel that the High Eldar living in Valinor, from whom these histories ultimately derived, must have known the 'true', scientific formation of the solar system, even if their traditions were later confused by the Elves and Men who transcribed and transmitted them. But most seriously of all, he felt that he could not 'make up [astronomically absurd] stories of that kind' in a world where everyone believes we live upon a spherical island in space. As he wrote tersely: 'you cannot do this any more'.

Christopher Tolkien comments: 'It seems to me that he was devising – from within it – a fearful weapon against his own creation.' It is sad to find Tolkien writing in his notes to himself that

> The Making of the Sun and Moon *must* occur long before the com-
> ing of the Elves; and *cannot* be made to be after the death of the
> Two Trees – if that occurred in any connexion with the sojourn of
> the Noldor in Valinor. The time allowed is too short. Neither could
> there be woods and flowers &c. on earth, if there had been no light
> since the overthrow of the Lamps!

The whole poetic conception of the mythology needed to be altered to accord with modern science. But that would have a knock-on effect, for even *The Lord of the Rings* was full of references to the earlier conception (such as the identity of Elrond's father with the planet Venus, the morning and evening star). As his son remarked, 'the old structure was too compre-hensive, too interlocked in all its parts, indeed its roots too deep, to with-stand such a devastating surgery' (p. 383).

Yet in fact, Tolkien being Tolkien, the fussy, incomplete revisions to his myths are more interesting than one might have imagined. The sheer size of the universe is further developed, and the 'centrality' of Arda is explained by the fact that it forms the appropriate stage setting for the great theologi-cal drama of the Children of God and the battle between Good and Evil. The sun is now intended from the start, and it is not kindled from the Golden Tree but hallowed by Varda with a 'holy light' from Ilúvatar. Melkor desires the new light and ravishes the divine maiden who inhabits the sun. Thereafter the sun is marred, the maiden departs, and the original plan of the Valar is spoiled. The importance of the Two Trees in later history is now explained by the fact that they were kindled before the rape of the sun, so that both they and the Silmarils contain part of the light given to it by Ilúvatar.

The greatest problems Tolkien was wrestling with at this time seemed to concern not the sun, but the moon and the stars, and the difficulty of preserving elements of the myth in which the special relationship of the Elves to the stars is established. He played with the idea of dark volcanic mists hiding the sun, and with the construction of a dome that would protect Arda (or at least Valinor) from Melkor, inlaid by Varda with the patterns of the stars in the universe outside. Nothing really resolved it, and the revision was never carried through.

In *The Voyage of the Dawn Treader* by C. S. Lewis, the boy Eustace objects to being told that he is meeting a retired star: 'In our world,' he says, 'a star is a huge ball of flaming gas.' The star replies, 'Even in your world, my son, that is not what a star is but only what it is made of.' I suspect that there is something truer in Tolkien's original mythological conception than anything that would have emerged from the later tinkering. But I may be wrong. Perhaps he was reaching for something he never attained, but could see in his mind's eye: a poetic revision of his cosmology that would assimilate modern science, and heal by a vision of beauty our culture that is so wounded by the severance of reason from imagination.

BIBLIOGRAPHY

Tolkien Sources

1. *The Lord of the Rings* (1954–5), *The Hobbit* (1937), and *The Silmarillion* (1977) by J. R. R. Tolkien are readily available in various editions, as are the essay 'On Fairy-Stories' (cited here from *The Monsters and the Critics and Other Essays*, edited by Christopher Tolkien, 1983) and 'Leaf by Niggle' (from *Tree and Leaf*, 1975)
2. *The Letters of J. R. R. Tolkien*, edited by Humphrey Carpenter (1981)
3. 'The History of Middle-Earth', Vols I–XII, edited by Christopher Tolkien (1983–96), especially Vols I and II (*The Book of Lost Tales*), Vol. V (*The Lost Road and Other Writings*), Vol. IX *(Sauron Defeated)*, and Vol. X (*Morgoth's Ring*)
4. *Unfinished Tales* by J. R. R. Tolkien (1980)

All the above are published currently and copyright © by HarperCollins in the UK and Houghton Mifflin in the USA. Dates are those of first publication.

The Letters of J. R. R. Tolkien

The following Letters in particular contain substantial material for the further exploration of Tolkien's oeuvre, its ramifications and significance – including its religious and spiritual dimension.

Letter 43 (see also 49). On women, marriage, chivalry and the Eucharist.

Letter 113. To Lewis, offering a rare insight into the friendship of the Inklings.

Letter 131. A detailed summary of his life's work.

Letter 142. In which he speaks of his Catholic inspiration.

Letters 144, 153–6. The metaphysical background, and answers to difficult questions.

Letter 163. His account to W. H. Auden of how he came to write the books.

Letter 181. About the quest and Frodo's 'failure'; on Elves as artists.

Letter 183. A detailed response to Auden's review; on politics, Good and Evil.

Letter 186. The various underlying themes and meaning of *The Lord of the Rings*.

Letter 183. On morality and politics (see also Letter 186).

Letter 200. About the 'gods' and their role in the story.

Letters 207, 210. Hilarious comments on the film 'treatment' proposed in 1957.

Letters 211–12. On the mythology and its purpose.

Letter 214. The traditions and social arrangements of Hobbits.

Letter 246. Frodo's 'failure' and fate.

Letter 297. On names in *The Lord of the Rings*, their origins and meaning.

Letter 306. On the state of the Church after Vatican II.

Letter 310. On the meaning of life, written to a schoolgirl.

Further Reading

Bradley J. Birzer, *J. R. R. Tolkien's Sanctifying Myth: Understanding Middle-Earth* (ISI Books, 2002)

Ian J. Boyd and Stratford Caldecott (eds), *A Hidden Presence: The Catholic Imagination of J. R. R. Tolkien* (Chesterton Press, 2003)

Humphrey Carpenter, *J. R. R. Tolkien: A Biography* (George Allen & Unwin, 1977)

Humphrey Carpenter, *The Inklings: C. S. Lewis, J. R. R. Tolkien, Charles Williams, and their Friends* (George Allen & Unwin, 1978)

Jane Chance, *Tolkien's Art: A Mythology for England*, revised edition (University Press of Kentucky, 2001)

Patrick Curry, *Defending Middle-Earth: Tolkien, Myth and Modernity* (Floris Books, 1999)

Verlyn Flieger, *Splintered Light: Logos and Language in Tolkien's World* (Eerdmans, 1983)

Verlyn Flieger, *A Question of Time: J. R. R. Tolkien's Road to Faërie* (Kent State University Press, 1997)

Verlyn Flieger and Carl F. Hostetter, *Tolkien's* Legendarium: *Essays on 'The History of Middle-Earth'* (Greenwood Press, 2000)

Timothy R. O' Neill, *The Individuated Hobbit: Jung, Tolkien and the Archetypes of Middle-Earth* (Houghton Mifflin, 1979)

Joseph Pearce, *Tolkien: Man and Myth* (HarperCollins, 1998)

Joseph Pearce (ed.), *Tolkien: A Celebration* (HarperCollins, 1999)

Richard Purtill, *J. R. R. Tolkien: Myth, Morality and Religion* (Ignatius Press, 2003)

Patricia Reynolds and Glen H. GoodKnight (eds), *Proceedings of the J. R. R. Tolkien Centenary Conference, Keble College 1992* (Tolkien Society/Mythopoeic Society, 1995)

T. A. Shippey, *The Road to Middle-Earth* (HarperCollins, 1992)

T. A. Shippey, *J. R. R. Tolkien: Author of the Century* (HarperCollins, 2000)

(Bibliographic details of works cited that are not directly about Tolkien or his work will be found in the Notes.)

Online Resources

The Tolkien Society: www.tolkiensociety.org/
The HarperCollins Tolkien web-site: www.tolkien.co.uk/index_nf.htm
The Encyclopedia of Arda: www.glyphweb.com/arda/default.htm
The Mythopoeic Society: www.mythsoc.org/

Sites Devoted to the Study of Tolkien's Invented Languages

www.elvish.org/
www.uib.no/People/hnohf/index.html

Sites for the Most Prominent Tolkien Illustrators

www.tednasmith.com
www.john-howe.com
www.dfxwebs.com/Artists/Lee
www.endicott-studio.com/biolee.html
www.eshrike.com/tolkien

Verlyn Flieger's Website

www.mythus.com/index.html

ΠOTES

Publisher details not given in the Notes will be found in the Bibliography.

Introduction

1. C. S. Lewis, *Of This and Other Worlds*, ed. Walter Hooper (Collins, 1982), p. 112.
2. The *Letters* are referred to by number rather than page, since page numbers vary between British and US editions. (Thus 'L 66' means Letter No. 66 on both sides of the Atlantic.)

Chapter 2: A Very Great Story

3. Humphrey Carpenter, *J. R. R. Tolkien: A Biography*, p. 89.
4. I owe this insight to Teresa Caldecott.
5. Carpenter, *J. R. R. Tolkien: A Biography*, p. 73.
6. C. S. Lewis, *The Abolition of Man* (HarperCollins, 1978), p. 48.

Chapter 3: A Hidden Presence: Tolkien's Catholicism

7. Flannery O' Connor, *Mystery and Manners,* ed. Sally and Robert Fitzgerald (Farrar, Straus & Giroux, 1962), pp. 173, 175.
8. Dwight Longenecker, *Adventures in Orthodoxy: The Marvels of the Christian Creed and the Audacity of Belief* (Sophia Institute Press, 2003), p. 51.
9. John Saward, *Cradle of Redeeming Love: The Theology of the Christmas Mystery* (Ignatius Press, 2002), pp. 320–21.
10. For Tolkien's own speculations about what might have happened if Frodo had challenged Sauron with the Ring, and how Elrond and Galadriel might have been corrupted by it, see the end of L 246.
11. And mushrooms, for some reason known only to Hobbits!

12. J-P. de Caussade, *Abandonment to Divine Providence* (Doubleday Image, 1975), p. 48.

13. *Unfinished Tales* contains a very moving story of an unhappy marriage – that of the voyager Aldarion, who became the sixth King of Númenor, and his wife Erendis.

14. He was also known as the Apostle of Confession, and indeed Tolkien would always try to receive the sacrament of reconciliation before Communion. For more on St Philip, read Paul Türks, *Philip Neri: The Fire of Joy* (T. & T. Clark, 1995).

15. Thérèse died of tuberculosis, and her last months were spent in physical and spiritual agony, not even consoled by her faith, for that was taken away from her or buried so deep that she was no longer conscious of it. In more recent times, Mother Teresa of Calcutta was revealed after her death to have spent most of her life deprived of the experience of faith, despite the fact that all through this time she radiated joy and hope to those around her. Jesus forsaken on the cross experienced all of this, and worse. Without him, this suffering, in which the saints have a share, would be nothing but evil. In him and with him, however, it is redemptive. It too becomes a sacrament, something both human and divine, joining man and God.

Chapter 4: Let These Things Be

16. G. K. Chesterton, *Saint Francis of Assisi*, in *The Collected Works of G. K. Chesterton*, Vol. II (Ignatius Press, 1986), p. 44.

17. Verlyn Flieger, *Splintered Light: Logos and Language in Tolkien's World* (Eerdmans, 1983), p. 57

18. Ibid. 'Be!' (*kun*) is also the first word of God to the creation according to the Koran.

19. J. H. Newman, *Parochial and Plain Sermons* (Ignatius Press, 1987), p. 453. In the creation story we find at the beginning of *The Silmarillion*, Tolkien makes a point of emphasising the continued active involvement of the angels in the World, 'which still the Ainur are shaping'.

20. See Lawrence D. Goodall, 'Of Universals, Angels, and Inklings', *Communio*, Fall 2002.

21. No account is given of the origin or nature of Tom Bombadil, though

he is described as the oldest of living beings on the earth. Perhaps he is the spirit of nature, a Maia of Yavanna, incarnating the vigour of spring and summer. Perhaps he is a spirit of laughter, the laughter of Tulkas the Strong. Perhaps he is simply music, for he seems incapable of speaking prose: his words dance in a rhythm and shade into song, and 'his songs are stronger songs'. The Ring has no power over him, cannot even make him invisible, for 'he is the master'.

22. But see 'The Tale of Adanel' at the end of the Notes on the 'Debate of Finrod and Andreth' (in *Morgoth's Ring*).

23. They lie, in fact, in an Oxford cemetery (see p. 99). The tale of Beren and Lúthien is a tale of grace. The 'Tale of the Children of Húrin' (see *Unfinished Tales*) is a contrasting story of 'dis-grace'. Set only a few years after the adventure of Beren, it concerns the destiny of Túrin Turambar, who marries his sister unawares and slays himself in grief. The tragedy unfolds under the eyes of his father, the hero Húrin, captured by Morgoth in the Battle of Unnumbered Tears and fixed in a high seat for his torment, as Morgoth demonstrates his power to doom Húrin's family to darkness and despair. There are few glimmers of hope in the story: Tolkien confronts the reality of evil unflinchingly. It is only in the context of the *legendarium* as a whole that we see how rare moments of radiance, swiftly swallowed, may outweigh the dark. In the tale of Beren and Lúthien, with the glimpse it affords us of the power of love to move the heart of Death himself, we sense the distant promise of redemption.

General Note for Chapter 4

In the Age of the Stars, the first Kings of the Elves were **Ingwë** (of the Vanya), **Elwë**/Thingol and **Olwë** (of the Teleri) and **Finwë** (of the Noldor). Having been shown the bliss and safety that awaits them in Aman, they lead their peoples into the West. Elwë remains behind: he marries **Melian** (of the divine race of Maia) and settles in Middle-earth, where their daughter **Lúthien** is born.

The Noldor: In Aman, Finwë is slain when Morgoth steals the Silmarils. Finwë's sons are **Fëanor** (by Miriel), **Fingolfin** and **Finarfin** (by Indis). Fëanor in turn has seven sons, Fingolfin three (including **Fingon** and **Turgon**), and Finarfin five (including **Finrod**/Felagund and **Galadriel**).

The Noldor return to Middle-earth out of the West in pursuit of the Silmarils.

Men: Men appear in the First Age of the Sun. The Edain or Elf-friends have three Houses: Beor, Hador and Haleth. **Beren**, who later marries Lúthien the daughter of Thingol, with whom he recovers a Silmaril from Morgoth, comes of the House of Beor. **Húrin** and **Huor**, and their respective sons **Túrin** (the tragic hero) and **Tuor** (the human messenger of Ulmo), come from the inter-marriage of the Second and Third Houses of the Edain.

The Half-Elven: The son of Beren and Lúthien is **Dior**, the first of the Half-Elven, the father of **Elwing**. Tuor marries **Idril**, the daughter of Turgon, King of Gondolin. Their child **Eärendil** marries Elwing, their sons being **Elrond** and **Elros** (the latter being appointed first King of Númenor). The two lines of descent from Eärendil are united again at the end of the Third Age by the marriage of **Arwen** the daughter of Elrond (her mother being the daughter of Galadriel) to **Aragorn** the descendent of Elros.

Chapter 5: Behind the Stars

24. John Saward explores this in *The Beauty of Holiness and the Holiness of Beauty* (Ignatius Press, 1997).

25. See also the author's footnote to the chronology in Appendix B of *The Lord of the Rings*, where he preserves the reference to Elanor's elvish looks.

26. Hans Urs von Balthasar, *The Glory of the Lord*, Vol. I (Ignatius Press, 1982), p. 153.

27. The passage I have just quoted has caused endless discussion among fans of the book and of the movie. Is the secret fire the same as the 'flame of Anor' or different? Some have thought that the latter is a reference to Gandalf's sword, Glamdring, which was once worn by King Turgon of Gondolin, but the word 'Anor' is obscure. It seems to be a variant of the Quenya name of the sun, Anar (as found in the name of the 'Tower of the Sun', Minas Anor, later renamed Minas Tirith or the Tower of Guard). In *Morgoth's Ring* (p. 44) Christopher Tolkien admits there is a puzzle about the word, for in some manuscripts Tolkien seemed to have used 'Anar' to refer to Eä or the World of Being. Despite this, it is reasonable to suppose that 'flame of Anor' is indeed an ancient Elvish name for Glamdring referring to the brightness of the blade, a

name that we surmise is known only to Gandalf (and perhaps the Balrog, who could well have been one of those who attacked Gondolin). After all, Gandalf cannot both 'serve' and 'wield' the Secret Fire itself.

28. This is not the place to delve into the many interpretations that have been offered of this passage and the biblical notion of Wisdom. For further theological illumination one might do well to turn to a French theologian who knew and admired Tolkien, Louis Bouyer, and particularly to his book *Cosmos: The World and the Glory of God* (St Bede's Publications, 1988), pp. 188–93.

29. Hans Urs von Balthasar, *The Glory of the Lord*, Vol. I (Ignatius Press, 1982), p. 441.

Appendices

30. John Ruskin, cited in James S. Taylor, *Poetic Knowledge: The Recovery of Education* (State University of New York Press, 1998), p. 116.

31. Timothy R. O' Neill, *The Individuated Hobbit,* p. 37.

32. Jacques Maritain, *Creative Intuition in Art and Poetry* (Harvill Press, 1954), p. 94.

İ П D E X